Praise for *Djinn*

"*Djinn* is an impressive memoir that shatters the stereotypical image of the Dutch Moroccan man. It's funny, gritty, sincere, and very touching."
— Nadia Bouras, Leiden University

"This important book provides not only a firsthand account of the coming-of-age of a queer Muslim—a contested identity to say the least—but also offers a much-needed exploration of the racism and Islamophobia behind the celebratory narrative of Dutch neoliberal multiculturalism."
— Fatima El-Tayeb, author of *European Others: Queering Ethnicity in Postnational Europe*

Djinn

SUNY SERIES IN QUEER POLITICS AND CULTURES

Cynthia Burack and Jyl J. Josephson, editors

TOFIK DIBI

Djinn

Translated and with an Introduction by
NICOLAAS P. BARR

For information, contact State University of New York Press, Albany, NY
www.sunypress.edu

Library of Congress Cataloging-in-Publication Data

Names: Dibi, Tofik, 1980- author.
Title: Djinn / Tofik Dibi ; translated by Nicolaas P. Barr.
Other titles: Djinn. English
Description: Albany : State University of New York Press, [2021] | Series: SUNY series in queer
    politics and cultures
Identifiers: LCCN 2020004577 | ISBN 9781438481302 (paperback) | ISBN
    9781438481319 (ebook)
Subjects: LCSH: Dibi, Tofik, 1980- | Gay men—Netherlands—Biography. | Gay leg-
    islators—Netherlands—Biography. | Muslim gays—Netherlands—Biography. |
    Moroccans—Netherlands—Biography. | Discrimination. | Human rights.
Classification: LCC HQ75.8.D53 A3 2021 | DDC 306.76/62092 [B]—dc23
LC record available at https://lccn.loc.gov/2020004577

10 9 8 7 6 5 4 3 2 1

Translator's Introduction

Tofik Dibi is best known in the Netherlands as a politician, rather than an author. He became a public figure in 2006, when he was unexpectedly elected to the Dutch Parliament at the mere age of twenty-six. As a Moroccan-Dutch Muslim man, he regularly faced off against some of the leading anti-Islam politicians and pundits who have dominated the Dutch landscape for the past two decades. A young, charismatic speaker, he was voted "political talent of the year" by the Dutch parliamentary press in 2008.

The media was captivated not just by Dibi's political abilities. Throughout his term in Parliament from 2006 to 2012, journalists speculated about his sexual orientation and pressured Dibi to confirm their suspicions that he was gay. Yet only with the original publication of *Djinn* in Dutch in 2015 did he define himself publicly as queer.

Djinn is both a personal and a political memoir. In taking us from his early childhood through his political career, Dibi traces his experience of conflict between his sexuality and his religious identity. In so doing, he also allows us to see pressing contemporary issues of immigration, racism, and homophobia in a novel light.

As the book moves from Amsterdam to New York City to Morocco and back, some details may be familiar to English-speaking readers, such as cultural references to American pop music. It also shows the far-reaching impact of the 9/11 terrorist attacks, and of the United States' political response to them. Other phenomena may be less familiar, particularly the book's portrayal of the Netherlands, which is often perceived on the international stage as being exceptionally progressive and tolerant. Dibi paints a more troubling picture. As the son of Moroccan immigrants, he faced a demand for cultural assimilation from a society that refused, and arguably still refuses, to recognize Muslims and people of color as equal citizens. In Dutch political debates, predominantly white commentators from across the spectrum continue to treat Dutch Muslims primarily as a problem to be solved.

◆ ◆ ◆

In the Netherlands, the historical roots of the alleged conflict between Islam and European values are much longer and more complex than most popular accounts suggest. In the early 1960s, the Dutch economy was booming, creating gaping labor shortages, especially in mining, textiles, and other heavy industries. Tens of thousands of so-called *gastarbeiders*, or guest workers, from Turkey and Morocco began migrating to the country to fill this gap. The need for labor was so great that the Dutch and Moroccan governments formalized a worker recruitment agreement in 1969, although by then, most Moroccan immigrants had come on their own to the Netherlands. Today, both first-generation immigrants and their descendants are usually referred to disparagingly as *allochtonen*, or "those of foreign origin," even though most of the second generation (and beyond) are born-and-raised Dutch citizens.[1] Over the past few decades, Islam has become perhaps the key issue in Dutch politics. LGBTQ rights have figured centrally in those debates in ways that may seem surprising and contradictory. Open hostility toward Dutch Muslims is often expressed under the banner of tolerance and progressive so-

---

1 Officially, the government's Central Bureau of Statistics replaced the noun *allochtoon* with the adjective *niet-westerse migratieachtergrond* or "non-Western migration background" in 2016. This phrase has gained some currency, but mainstream language continues to reinforce the native/foreign distinction as a racial binary.

cial values. The Netherlands was the first country in the world to legalize same-sex marriage, in 2001, and respect for LGBTQ rights has become a component of the government's official integration exam.[2] The false assumption underlying this integration policy is that LGBTQ rights are wholly cherished by the (white) native Dutch population and must be defended against supposedly unenlightened immigrants—especially Muslims.

While we often associate support for LGBTQ rights with the left end of the political spectrum, in the Netherlands, politicians have long used the defense of those rights as the basis for right-wing, anti-Muslim rhetoric and policies. In the late 1990s, the Dutch politician Pim Fortuyn (an openly gay, formerly Marxist sociology professor) built much of his political platform on the defense of gay rights against the perceived threat of Muslims. Fortuyn was murdered in 2002 (by a white animal rights activist), but many of his ideas were taken up by the politician Geert Wilders, who founded a new right-wing party, Partij voor de Vrijheid or "Party for Freedom" (PVV), in 2004. Wilders has referred to Moroccan-Dutch people as "scum" and proposes mass deportations of Muslims, banning the Koran, and closing mosques. In line with Fortuyn's politics, the 2012 PVV electoral program stated, "We defend our gays against advancing Islam,"[3] which presupposes that gay people and Muslims are mutually exclusive groups.

◆ ◆ ◆

Dibi's personal narrative takes place against this historical and political background. He was born in 1980, in the small southwestern coastal city of Vlissingen, and his parents were part of the wave of immigration from Morocco in the decades prior. It was the rise of

---

2 Gloria Wekker, *White Innocence: Paradoxes of Colonialism and Race* (Durham, NC: Duke University Press, 2016), 7, and chapter 4.

3 Quoted in Wekker, *White Innocence*, 110.

anti-Muslim sentiment that sparked Dibi's engagement with politics. As a Member of Parliament, his public visibility allowed him to be a sharp, dissenting voice to Geert Wilders and other politicians, and to defend religious freedom and rights—not only for Dutch Muslims and other minorities, but for all Dutch people. As a member of the Green-Left Party, which is thoroughly secular and committed to the principle of religious freedom and equality before the law, Dibi saw his political role as advocating for the rights of both religious believers and nonbelievers to live as they choose, as protected by Article 1 of the Dutch constitution, which prohibits discrimination on any grounds.[4]

As *Djinn* makes clear, however, Dibi's personal relationship to the wider Muslim community was also a fraught one. As a gay man, he worried about not only the fate of his political career but also the possibility being ostracized by his family and the wider community if his sexuality were revealed. It is important to remember, though, that these fears and risks are common to queer people in heteronormative communities worldwide. And racist stereotypes about Muslim homophobia serve as an all-too-convenient excuse to ignore ongoing issues of homophobia in white populations.

In fact, conversations about LGBTQ issues have been underway among European Muslims for decades, and as with other communities, attitudes toward sexual identity continue to become more

---

4 There are roughly a dozen political parties in the Dutch Parliament, ranging from far left to far right. Anti-Muslim political positions are more common on the right, but these issues have also created fault lines on the liberal and left ends of the spectrum—particularly around perceived concerns about feminism and LGBTQ rights. See Sara R. Farris, *In the Name of Women's Rights: The Rise of Femonationalism* (Durham, NC: Duke University Press, 2017).

open, especially among younger generations.[5] More fundamentally, Muslims in Europe—not to mention in the United States—deserve not mere "tolerance," but rather equal rights and recognition of the full complexity of their identities. Dibi's story invites us to rethink the simplistic categories that we so often use to define people along the lines of race, religion, and sexuality, and instead take inspiration from his challenging path toward self-definition.

---

5 See Fatima El-Tayeb, *European Others: Queering Ethnicity in Postnational Europe* (Minneapolis: University of Minnesota Press, 2011), chapter 4, and the current work of the Amsterdam-based queer Muslim association Stichting Maruf (www.maruf.eu).

Djinn

✦

O-o-h child things are gonna get easier, keep, keep ya head up,
o-o-h child things'll get brighter, keep ya head up
—TUPAC SHAKUR,
"KEEP YA HEAD UP"

Foreword

The most terrifying monsters are monsters that you never see, not even for a fraction of a second. They are whispered about, and you know that they're there, but they remain invisible. In my early years, I devoured horror films, from classics like *The Shining* and *Carrie* to absurd B movies about carnivorous plants and murderous cars. There weren't any films that scared the shit out of me as much as the ones with lurking monsters—sowing death and destruction but never actually seen.

Even more terrifying is when the monster is not only formless, but also voiceless. Then no one knows what it is and what it wants, and the image of the monster becomes even more grotesque. Only evil itself can have no face and no voice.

It works just like that in real life. The Dominican-American author Junot Díaz once told a group of students—children of immigrants like me—his motivation for becoming a writer.

> You guys know about vampires? [...] You know, vampires have no reflections in a mirror? There's this idea that monsters don't have reflections in a mirror. And what I've always thought isn't that monsters don't have reflections in a mirror. It's that if you want to make a human being into a monster, deny them, at the cultural level, any reflection of themselves. And growing up, I felt like a monster in some ways. I didn't see myself reflected at all. I was like, "Yo, is something wrong with me? That the whole society seems to think that people like me don't exist?"

For most of my life, I haven't seen myself reflected. Not in my family, not in my circle of friends, not in school or on the block, and not in books, films, or TV series. Even now, I seldom recognize myself. I have long thought that people like me didn't exist, and that meant that I couldn't exist. Not fully, in any case. I have written this book in order to no longer feel invisible. It is my heartfelt wish that it helps others to be able to see themselves.

✦ ✦ ✦

For my brothers and sisters.

They say that falling stars are nocturnal projectiles that are fired from the heavens upon djinns. If that's true, the heavens can shine with pride tonight. They also say that you can make a wish if you see a falling star. If that's true, I wish desperately to find a way out of here. I swear that this really is the last time.

I can't see my face in the mirror of my hotel room. I'm somewhere under the swelling that has deformed the area around my eyes. How will I get rid of it in time? I have to be back in the Tweede Kamer, the Dutch Parliament. How am I going to solve it this time? I think my ribs are bruised.

"You deserve it."

There *they* are. A soon as *it* does something, *they* attack. If it goes wrong, *they* are merciless.

"Your fault."

They are proven right again. Things went badly again. Because of *it*. *It* has been with me for as long as I can remember. *It* accompanies me wherever I go. *It* has no name. If I give *it* a name, *it* becomes tangible, but without one, *it* remains elusive. Nameless or not, *it* cannot be suppressed. However hard I keep praying that *it* will disappear, *it* always finds its way back.

Where *it* is, *they* are. *They* also accompany me everywhere. *It* and *they* have been at war for a long time. *It* is alone. *They* are many. *They* have not one, but many, many names. *They* are the neighbors, the butcher, my cousins, my aunts and uncles. *They* are my fellow

Muslims, colleagues, and classmates. My favorite movies and TV series. Loose acquaintances, and that group of boys on the street corner. *They* are *the people*. And *the people* fear and hate *it*.

It and *they* both live within me. As long as *it* lies low, *they* keep a reasonable distance. But as soon *it* becomes restless, I hear *them* march. About six months ago, I became a member of Parliament (MP) for GroenLinks, the Green-Left Party. Immediately, *they* grew in number: party members, other politicians, journalists, voters, internet trolls, the Moroccan-Dutch community. The army of *them* is now so big that *it* is more hopeless than ever before.

Indeed, it seemed that way, but after everything that's happened, I should have known that it wouldn't be that easy. MP or not, *it* lurks from a distance, waiting for a moment of weakness, and strikes. This is one of those moments. It's the May recess, and I'm in New York. I can do that easily now—book a flight to a faraway metropolis. When I got my first paycheck, I took my suitcase to Schiphol Airport on a whim and traveled to Cuba, because once, when I was broke, I had seen on a travel show that you could swim with dolphins there. This coming summer, I want to take my mother and brothers to Morocco, because we haven't been there in so long. Then we can also go to the edge of the Sahara, where my father is buried.

So much has changed now that I'm an MP. I've gone from eviction notices and having the gas and electricity shut off to having a whole lot of money. Everyone in the neighborhood thinks that I've become a millionaire, or a wandering employment agency. My mother keeps asking if I have work for people from my community, and sometimes she brings a CV along herself: "Tofik, if you have time, take a look and see if you can line something up for Issam, Nadya's son. He's graduated and really wants to work."

Now and then I stop by a random ATM, even when I don't need cash, just to press the "check balance" button. Even after all the bills have been paid, there's still at least a thousand euros in the account.

It feels exactly like the first time I got an allowance, of one guilder per week.

New York is the place where *it* had the courage to *do* something for the first time, instead of just thinking about it. That was five years ago, shortly after 9/11. *Here I am again.* It's the May recess, and there's an ocean between *it* and *them*—maybe *it* can even happen again? Come on, who am I kidding ... I've come back here for only one reason.

The hotel where I'm staying, the Carter, is shabby, and a couple minutes' walk from Times Square. Since it's cheap, people check in and out constantly. Strangers' faces disappear as quickly as they appear. The anonymity fuels *its* courage. There are four computers in the hotel lobby where you can access the internet for a couple bucks. I feel it immediately when I see them: the tingling irresistibility of the Web, where *it* is powerful and *they* are weak. There, I can do everything I want, and feel everything as who I really am. And, here, I don't need to look constantly over my shoulder like I do at my regular spot in Amsterdam. I take my things to my room and immediately take a seat behind a computer. What were the good chat rooms again? I google for a bit, find something on Yahoo! that I had looked at earlier, and go in. It starts right away: "What do you look like?" "What are you looking for?" "What do you like?" "Where are you?" "Do you travel or host?" "Do you have a photo?" All of the standard questions come up. After a few hours, it looks like there's someone with the profile I'm looking for: someone with the same internal war, someone dealing with *it* and *them*. That's what ultimately tips the scales. I need that connection.

I need to get to the Bronx. It's already almost midnight. I take a quick shower, throw on my jeans, sneakers, and black leather jacket, and hop in a cab. It still feels like that first time, grabbing one of these yellow taxis. I read the address that I scribbled on a piece of paper. It's a ways from Manhattan to the Bronx. The driver tries to make small talk, but I ignore him as politely as possible. I'm ashamed that

I've flown thousands of miles, only to fall back into old, unhealthy temptations.

We're here. It's a long, deserted street with fairly large white houses, each with a car parked in front. I get out of the cab, walk to the house, and then it begins. *It* and *they* mentally attack each other. Psychological warfare.

"You'll never break the habit." "You're an MP now. What are you doing?" "What if someone finds out?"

This always happens right in front of the door. *They* know exactly what *they* need to say to sow doubt. *They* flash by in my head: my mother, who is worried about my safety; kids on the block, pointing and cursing; the fathers at the mosque on the August Allebé Square who want to protect me from Satan; my favorite singers, who celebrate love between men and women in their songs; and members of my family in Morocco, who simply don't understand. In the Netherlands, I've often turned around because of this. Now I'm far from home, far from *the people*. I don't know what it is: lust, hunger for affection, distance, something else, but *it* wins this battle. I walk up the steps to the front door. My heart races and bounces in my throat, no matter how often I've done this before. The sexual tension during the chat has turned into short-breathed angst. The door is cracked, and it's dark inside.

"Hello?"

It's quiet for a bit.

"Come on in."

I walk inside, but there's something off. The voice I hear is of an older person. Everything is so dark, and I can only see a silhouette. That's someone different from who I talked to in the chat room. My eyes still haven't adjusted to the dark, so I can't see clearly. But I need to get out of here.

"Sorry, I think I'm gonna go...."

A hand grabs me by the collar. I step back in fear. The back of my head hits something angular by the door and I stumble, but I don't fall all the way to the ground. I try to push myself up and turn toward the door. Two hands grab me—one by the arm, the other on my leg. I still can't see well.

"Please, I need to go," I say weakly. "My friend has this address ... I always make sure someone knows where I'm going if I do something like this ..."

I can feel my clothes being pulled. I try to slow things down but get punched in the face. This is serious. My pants get pulled down. I try to stop it, but it doesn't work. I still can't see well in the dark. One shoe comes off, and I pull my other foot away quickly. If I don't struggle, I won't get hit again, he says. I gesture like I'm submitting.

I try to make a fake move and run to the door, but before I take one step, I'm thrown to the ground in a single movement. I feel a punch. Another one. There goes my other shoe, and my pants follow. I hear muffled sounds, but I'm no longer there. I already know what's going to happen. This isn't the first time. I disappear into myself, away from here, to a place where everything makes sense.

I'm with my father, my mother, and my brothers. We're driving toward Morocco in a caravan of fully packed cars and vans, with curtains blocking the sun. Jamal, Abdelaziz, Nourdin, and I sit in the backseat, whining for the windows to be opened farther, and Mom and Dad ignore us in the front. In the cooler, there are boxes of apple juice, peanut butter sandwiches, and, of course, Heinz Ketchup and Remia Mayonnaise to eat with French fries in Morocco, because they don't have those sauces there. The suitcases are packed to the max: they're crazy for Dutch goods in Morocco. Every once in a while, we stop to eat with the other families and to give the fathers a break from driving. The butane stove is used to make tea or coffee. Usually after the first day of the trip, we lose track of the other families and take off on our own, just the six of us. The coolest part is when we get to the winding roads through the forests in France. In the distance, there are isolated, illuminated houses visible through the trees. They make me think of the edible house made of candy, *speculaas*, and pancakes in Hansel and

Gretel. I point to one of the houses and begin to tell my brothers an improvised version of the fairy tale. I have so much fun, because they always get scared when I get to the witch. When it really gets scary, they beg me to stop. As soon as night falls and the cold slowly creeps up from underneath the car, from our feet up to our heads, we fall asleep one by one, like dominoes. I try to stay awake the longest, partly to help Dad stay awake. He might fall asleep at the wheel. Everything is perfect in this moment. Someday I want a family like this, with a mother, father, and children, the way it's supposed to be.

For a moment, I think there are raindrops hitting the windshield, but they are beads of sweat landing on my body. The muffled sounds become clearer, and the stabbing pain in my ribs and face sharper. I don't know if I should try to break free. Maybe I should try to talk instead—convince him, like in a debate. Say that I don't want this and that I won't cause any problems if I can leave. I'm a good talker.

"I won't tell anyone...." Before I can finish the sentence, a white pillow is pushed onto my face. This is to scare me, to subdue me definitively, I'm sure. I put both of my hands in the air as a sign of surrender, but the pillow is pushed even harder onto my face. I can't breathe anymore. I try to free my legs, but it's impossible. I try to give a signal with my hands again, in vain. Is this it? Is it going to happen this time? Is this the end? And just when I finally have something to lose.

At first everything was black, and now everything is turning white. Are the ice crystals coming, the blue after the white?

The pillow comes off. I don't move. I breathe deeply but carefully —anything to prevent another outburst. I lie there and stare at hell; he is leaking sweat as hot as lava.

It's over.

I can see better in the dark now, but I avoid eye contact. Ashamed, I look for my things and walk to the door. I get dressed, half inside and half in front of the door. Then I start to run. The street is still deserted. I grab the first taxi I can. The driver watches me in the rearview mirror for the entire ride.

"You didn't really fight back, Tofik ... he probably thought you wanted it."

In the hotel lobby, everyone is looking at me. I don't look back, because otherwise I'll lose my concentration. I walk with purpose. It's the only thing keeping me from crying. At the elevator, someone asks me if I'm all right. "I'm okay, thank you," I reply. I almost lose my concentration but control myself just in time. In my hotel room, after I look at myself in the mirror, I see two big white pillows that make me think of the darkness. I put them away, grab a sweater from my suitcase, and lie down on it. I fall asleep immediately.

In the morning, I recognize my face even less than the night before. I walk straight to the computers in the lobby. Google is my friend, I think to myself. I look up remedies for black eyes and bruised ribs. Around the corner from the hotel, I pick up a bunch of ointments and painkillers at Duane Reade.

By evening, the tiny sliver of peace that my Google crisis plan had brought me is gone. I can't think of anything else than the computers in the lobby, and the Yahoo! chat room. He'll lay low for a bit after what he's done, but you never know. I log in, scan all of the people online, and see his name there.

Yes! Okay, now what?

In a single breath, a feeling of triumph, disbelief, and powerlessness. What should I actually say? Should I curse? Or ask him why he did it? The nerve, sitting here chatting away as if nothing happened. Or is there really an issue? Did I do this to myself? I'm going to scare him—I'll say that I'm going to report him, that he picked the wrong person to mess with. I'll let him beg for forgiveness. While I'm thinking about this, I hear *them* whispering in my head: "Can you imagine the headlines in the Netherlands?"

I double-click on his name to open a chat window and say hello. He says "hi" back. I wait for more, but there's nothing. No "sorry," nothing.

"Do you think you're gonna get away with this?"

"What are you talking about?"

I swear, if he were standing in front of me now and I had a knife in my hand, I would cut his throat.

"I will make you pay for what you did."

Bloop.

He's logged off.

With sunglasses from Chinatown to camouflage the black eyes, I spend the rest of the recess smearing ointments and downing vitamin C. I maneuver around people to avoid contact with my ribs. Day by day the swelling is going down, and the blue, purple, green, and yellow hues fade away. Only my ribs are still painful, and I have wounds that no one sees.

Sometimes I visit the Hangar on Christopher Street for a couple of fruity cocktails. The Wizard of Oz that I met my first time here doesn't work here anymore, sadly. Now and then someone asks me what happened to my face. I always come up with a falling-down-the-stairs line, and it's always followed by the I-don't-believe-that-at-all-but-I'm-not-going-to-say-anything look.

The flight back to the Netherlands is approaching, and every day there's less to see on my face. Only my ribs still hurt. I feel proud—proud that I've solved this again on my own.

He just logged off.

Disappeared with the click of a button.

Bloop.

Not long after I've returned to our faction in the Parliament, Femke, our chairwoman, and Tom, our political adviser, ask to talk to me; by the tone of their voices, I can tell it's something serious. *De Telegraaf* is working on a story about me. It feels like the whole world is crumbling under my feet.

Could the newspaper know what happened in New York? How is that possible? Or do they know about the previous times? About before?

I really look up to Femke and Tom. They're the only ones in our party's faction that I'm really a bit intimidated by. When I look at their combined mental powers, it's as if I see Professor Xavier, the telepathic, gifted founder of the X-Men, in front of me. I don't want them to perceive a moment of weakness in me, so I react as nonchalantly as possible. They need to know that I'm strong.

When they reveal what the story is that the newspaper wants to publish, it turns out to be a fabrication from "an anonymous source" that claims I made out with a man in a restroom of the Parliament. I feel relieved and stressed at the same time: relieved because I know it's not true, and stressed, because the truth will always lose out if the lie is more entertaining.

Femke and Tom's advice echoes in my head: "Whatever you do, don't lie." They emphasize that no one can make me talk about personal issues that I don't want to talk about. I have the feeling they don't entirely believe me, that they think it's actually true. Of course, they suspect *it* as much as everyone else.

The gossip from *De Telegraaf* is hanging over me like a black cloud. It's nerve-wracking. It comes to a climax when the reporter who is working on the story waits for me at the plenary hall, with the cameras rolling. I try to escape into a debate hall that they're not allowed into without a pass, but they wait. They follow me to my office, with loud accusations that I'm not being honest about who I am. I'm so embarrassed about all of the staff and colleagues overhearing this racket. The newspaper ultimately doesn't publish this story, but it soon becomes clear that this is just the first of countless experiences with journalists from all kinds of media who try to expose *it* through lying or sneaky tricks.

I promise myself to be as good an MP as possible, to master the political handiwork, as Femke keeps telling me to do, in the hope that all of the attention will go toward those skills instead. I suppress what happened during the recess. But every now and then, I see the man's face in front of me.

I am happy—so happy—that he didn't kiss me. Even though no one was watching.

2

She sounds like an animal. I'm the first to wake up from her screams, because I only just fell asleep. Ever since I saw *A Nightmare on Elm Street* with Dad, I've tried to postpone falling asleep as long as possible so that Freddy Krueger can't catch me in my dreams.

I often watch movies late at night with my dad. When he sends us to bed, I always wait for my little brothers and my older brother to go up the stairs first while I stall for as long as possible. From the stairs, there's a perfect view of the couch in the living room, where Dad always ends his day. I give him a wishful look, as a signal that I want to stay up. By his facial expression, I can tell whether or not he's going to let me come down. If he frowns, it's a no. But usually he doesn't. Usually he ignores me for a bit, until he can't suppress smiling because of how eager I am. That's the sign I'm aiming for. When I sense that the others have fallen asleep, I tiptoe downstairs and climb onto the couch next to him. We've watched a lot of movies together, including some that I really shouldn't be allowed to see at my age.

Dad has a daily evening ritual in the Moroccan section of the living room. All of the Moroccan families in our town—there aren't many in Vlissingen—have a living room that is furnished on one side in typical Moroccan style and on the other in typical Dutch style. We're not allowed to sit in the Dutch section; it's reserved for special occasions. When we sit there, on a green velvet couch decorated with oak armrests, everyone is trying to act all sophisticated. It's our way of saying: "Look at us, we can be properly Dutch too, you know." Dad's

ritual consists of Van Nelle rolling tobacco—the extra strong one—
and tea. Not just any tea, but tea as it's prepared in the Sahara, where
he's from. "Moroccan whiskey" it's called, because of the strong, bitter
flavor in a small dose. In order to prove to him that I'm worthy company, I pretend that I like it too. I hardly drink any of it, but I make
long slurping sounds with every sip. At a certain point, after watching
a movie, he realizes that my glass is still full and stops serving it to me.

I wonder what the screaming is about and walk toward the stairs
all dizzy. He's not in the spot where he always sits. The scream comes
from the living room—it's my stepmother. Dad just married her, and
since she's been around, a couple of months now, we don't watch movies together anymore. She keeps screaming "El ghaddar!" which means
"traitor." My brothers—little Nourdin and soccer player Jamal—are
standing by my side on the stairs. She won't stop screaming. She's
calling him a traitor because they've just gotten married, and already
he's deserted her. He isn't saying anything back.

We walk slowly down the stairs and into the living room.
Everything seems normal, except for Dad. His "whiskey" and tobacco are on the table, but he's lying on his back on the floor. He's staring
up at the heavens. It looks as if there are ice crystals descending on
his face. They're turning his skin bluer and bluer, as though the stars
are preparing to make him one of them.

I hear muffled sounds in the background: the doorbell rings, and
people come inside. But I only see Daddy's chest. It's not moving up
and down anymore. Or is it? I stare at it, but I'm not sure of what I'm
seeing. Sometimes I see a motion, sometimes I don't. I try to move his
chest with my mind—telekinesis, it's called. I've been practicing it for
a while, ever since I read *Mathilda* by Roald Dahl. It's not working.

Or is it?

Then the muffled sounds become clearer. It sounds like someone
is crying, but it's not coming from children or from a woman. I only
know the sound of women and children crying. I see two of Daddy's
good friends standing behind him. They look like him, with remnants

of what were once full black and brown heads of hair, sideburns, deeply unbuttoned shirts, and flared pants. They are looking at him and crying. I've never seen Moroccan men cry—I thought they didn't do stuff like that.

After a while, sirens drown out the crying. The ambulance is here. The paramedics put him in a body bag and disappear into the night. Our neighbors have woken up from the noise and come to the door. They invite us to play Pac-Man on their personal computer. Dad was almost going to buy us a Nintendo—he just needed to save a little more money. Maybe when he comes back? It's important that he comes back. The movie that we watched a while ago is haunting me, and I feel like he knows what *it* is and what I need to do about it.

When I walk to school the next morning, I bump into my brother Aziz, who is a year younger than I am. He spent the night at Indio's house—a Ghanaian buddy. I don't know what to say, so I just keep walking. Everyone at school is staring at me. Someone told them what happened—I don't know who. I don't make eye contact, or else I'll break my concentration: I've been concentrating really hard since last night. I need to, or I'll start crying. If I do that, it's like admitting that something terrible has happened. The teacher calls me into his office after class. He tells me that his wife also lost her father at a young age, and how difficult that was for her. "Condolences," I say. I learned that word last night when I heard the neighbors say it. The teacher looks at me strangely. I almost lose my concentration but catch myself just in time.

When I'm home, someone rings the doorbell. It's my sister Malika. She lives with my brother Pascal at their mother Corrie's. Corrie was my father's Dutch girlfriend before he married my mother. Malika starts crying as soon as she comes inside. It's becoming increasingly difficult to keep my concentration. Malika is very tough: she plays soccer for VC Vlissingen, uses a lot of hairspray, and wears cool white-washed ripped jeans. I've wanted those ever since I watched *Grease* with Dad.

A bit later, we walk with a group of Moroccans from Vlissingen—friends and acquaintances of my father and mother—to an unfamiliar place that I don't like. Dad is lying here. An old friend of my mother's says to my brothers and me that we need to give him a kiss. I really don't want to, because everyone is watching.

At home, nothing seems right anymore. My stepmother becomes more and more physical. She was a teacher in Morocco, so she is adept at corporal punishment. Her hands seem built for it: wide, with short, thick fingers. With her green eyes, she reminds me of the evil stepmother in *Snow White*. Sometimes she hits so hard that she leaves bruises on my arms and legs. One time, during one of her fits, my brothers and I ducked behind my older brother Jamal, the soccer player. He protected his face with his hands and bent-up knees. She missed her target a couple of times, which infuriated her even more. The frustration of those misses culminated in one last, extra-fierce blow. Jamal raised one knee again to where her hand would land, and it clashed with her wrist. It didn't hurt him one bit, but she sprang back from the pain like a hissing cat. After that, we hid behind his soccer legs more often.

Since we never cry over our father in front of her, she starts calling us "*Yehud,*" or "Jews," as a slur. To avoid being around her, I play outside more, even though I'd much rather stay inside to draw and write. Every day, going home from the playground before it gets dark becomes a greater ordeal. It gets to the point where the four of us are seriously discussing the option of running away. We ask Ender, a Turkish kid in the neighborhood, for advice. His parents were good friends of my father and mother. The bottom line is we're too scared to run away, out of fear that if we're found, we'll be taken back home because no one will believe us. My stepmother can act her ass off when others are around. Heavyhearted, we walk home, while Ender makes jokes to cheer us up.

The only bright spot is that she hasn't lived in the Netherlands long enough to get a residency card, so she's desperately looking for a new husband. It takes up so much of her time and energy that she pays less attention to us. Sometimes she takes us with her on her dates, because she doesn't want to leave us home alone. She warns us that she'll kick our asses if we tell our Moroccan friends. One of her dates is a white dentist. He gives her a ring, but we never see him after that. When a few of her Moroccan friends are over, Nourdin and I accidentally mention the ring. When they're gone, she comes after us—even Nourdin, who is still very young. She's never been this vile. I swear, I want nothing more than to jump on her back and pull the hair out of her head until it bleeds. But she is strong and stout, and she hits hard when she goes berserk.

A while later, she meets a Jordanian man. He lives in Middelburg and sort of resembles Dad. We go to his place. I like that, because in his presence, she's more Snow White than evil stepmother. She acts so sweet and cool around him that I almost fall for it. When they take us to a shopping center that Dad used to take us to, I ask her if we can have some ice cream. I know she can't refuse, like she normally does, because he's there. We get the ice cream, and at home, I get a phenomenal beating. My father left her with debts, she says after the beating. We can't afford extras.

The Jordanian feels like a savior. He teaches me to play chess, and his daughters, from a previous marriage with a white woman, take us to McDonald's for the first time in our lives—the McDrive, no less, which is brand new in town. His daughters even give us an allowance of one guilder a week. Until that moment, I had only gotten a guilder once before in my life, when I left a baby tooth under my pillow. Dad said the tooth fairy left it there. We're so happy we tell our stepmother about the pocket money. She immediately takes it from us.

Fortunately, it won't take long before the big day arrives, the day we will learn whether we can live with our mom or have to stay with our stepmother. When our parents divorced, we wanted to stay with Dad, because our school and friends were there. Now we just want to get the hell out of here. A couple of people who work for chil-

dren's services ask us who we want to live with, and we all say "Mom!"
Shortly after, we get the news that Mom has been awarded custody.
I've asked Allah to save us from that bitch's clutches so often. I knew
He would come through.

Everything changes in a heartbeat. I can't even go and see Krispijn,
my best friend. I wanted to say goodbye to his pet stick insects. The
hardest part is not being able to see the Jordanian's daughters. One
of them has cancer. She is such a sweetheart. I just know she'll go
directly to heaven.

We drive home, hurry to pack some of our things, and walk to the
car. My stepmother is standing in front of the door. I let my brothers go ahead and take really slow steps. I'm mustering up the courage
to cuss her out before I never see her again. She needs to know how
despicable she is. I'm trying hard, but nothing comes out. I'm too
scared of her. The engine starts. I can't bear that she's standing there
like that, but we drive away.

She disappears from sight.

There's something else. Since that night, I went looking for my
father every day after school, but I still haven't found him. I don't
believe he's really gone. This move is ruining my search. One time, I
almost got him. I see a Moroccan man in a Mercedes, my father's favorite car, but when I run to the window, it turns out to be a stranger.
Such a shame—I would have loved to bring him to my brothers and
sister as a surprise. Amsterdam is better for now though. Anything
is better than living with that evil witch. I'll come up with an idea to
come back later and look for Dad.

With one tap on the gas pedal, she vanishes.

Poof.

I remember one time, when I was drawing something, the witch
came and sat next to me—something she never did. She told me that
he had come into our bedroom that night to give each of us a kiss. I
wanted nothing more than to believe her, but I don't trust her. I need
to find him. I need to know why he let me watch that movie that

night. *My Beautiful Laundrette*, it's called. It's about Omar, the son of a Pakistani man, Hussein Ali, who's down on his luck. Dad's name is also Hussein, but spelled differently. Omar wants to become rich, like everyone else in London, so his father asks his brother Nasser, a wealthy businessman, to help them out. For the sake of loyalty to family, he gives Omar a chance: he can run his filthy laundromat. Omar patches up the place with Johnny, an old buddy from school. Johnny needs all the help he can get, too, so together they try to make something out of the laundromat.

Dad is really into the film, more so than he normally is. Maybe because the story is also about racism: the guys that Johnny used to hang out with, a group of neo-Nazis, aren't too happy about his contact with Omar. Once we also had a terrible dispute with neighbors who didn't want us to live in their neighborhood. They threw a rock at our car and broke the window. They yelled awful things at my mother. Dad kept a gun in the car at the time. Sometimes I ran into their son and daughter on the way to school. We gave each other dirty looks; I don't know why exactly.

I really like the movie up until the point when, out of nowhere, Johnny pulls Omar into a dark alley and kisses him on the mouth. I look away quickly, like I always do so when someone's kissing on TV. It's kind of a Moroccan thing—some sort of antikissing reflex. It works like this: whoever is sitting closest to the remote grabs it as quickly as possible, preferably before the lips make contact. The rest automatically look in the other direction. Everyone stares at a different corner of the room; eye contact is avoided at all costs, giggling too. When the remote-control holder clicks back to the channel, everyone acts like nothing happened and continues to watch.

That's not what happens this time. Dad doesn't pick up the remote, even though it's sitting right next to him. I don't understand. I try to act as normal as possible so he doesn't notice anything. I'm completely disoriented. Then it happens again. Omar and Johnny are all over each other in a back room of the laundromat. The antikiss reflex seems to be malfunctioning. Dad keeps watching and doesn't click away. I want to run upstairs to my bed, but then he'll know something is up. I sit still and hold my breath, while inside, a hurricane rages. They're doing really crazy things. Omar's uncle comes into the room just when they're putting on their clothes. Omar thinks up an excuse, but Nasser doesn't believe him. He bows his head and leaves.

I have no idea what the rest of the movie looks like. I'm sitting on the couch, but I'm no longer there. I disappear into myself, far away from here. Why did Omar's uncle walk away like that? Did they do something wrong? Otherwise he wouldn't be disappointed, right? Why did Dad let me watch all of this? Isn't what Omar and Johnny were doing weird? Why were they doing that? Why couldn't I keep my eyes off of them? What was that feeling inside of me? Why did Dad act so normal? I don't understand any of this. I'll bring up the movie another time so that he can maybe explain it to me. It's as if he knows what *it* is.

We've arrived in Amsterdam. I can barely believe my eyes. Trams run through the streets, and there are people of color everywhere. Everything is so exciting. Dad would love this.

The most, most important thing is that I gave him a kiss. Even though everyone was watching.

3

My new school is called the Mercator School, and it's a two-minute walk from where we live now. Ria, our neighbor who lives in an apartment below us, has registered us for school, so they know that we're coming today. I hope they got it right. I would hate to have to go in front of the class and explain who I am and why I've come to the school so late in the year.

It's a "black" school, Ria says, which means that there are many immigrant children. She is a dear friend of my mom. She helps us with things like translating mail and stuff. Ria lives with Joop and their kids, Johan and Jolanda. They have two large, gray dogs. The immigrants in the neighborhood are afraid of the dogs. Joop is like the Hulk: big mouth, small heart, and, always, a visible butt crack. I'm so happy that we know them.

It takes a while to find the classroom for fifth grade in the chaos of kids, who look like they've escaped from a ratchet version of a United Colors of Benetton poster. At my old Catholic school, they would have had to write at least a hundred lines as punishment for their rebelliousness. I don't see Jamal and Aziz anywhere. I find my classroom, and thank God, the door is still open. I try to sneak in without anyone noticing me, but right before I find an empty seat, I hear: "Your dick or your life!"

I have absolutely no idea what that means. It comes from a tall, light-skinned kid with curly hair. The teacher isn't here yet. The classroom is buzzing. Everyone is looking at me, grinning and waiting to see how I'll react. I don't say a thing and manage to grab the first empty chair I can find, next to a Moroccan girl with a ponytail so long that it could almost be used as a broom. The class is littered with craft projects and drawings that hurt my eyes. When Teacher Thea walks in and takes attendance, it turns out that the light-skinned boy is named Hannibal. Teacher Thea is one of two Surinamese teachers at the school. She reminds me a little bit of MTV's animated character Daria, just with darker skin. Zubair warns me that she and Teacher Sally are lethal, so I'd better watch out. Zubair is one of the three Pakistani brothers at the school; the other two are Humair and Numair. They're really cool. I've never met Pakistanis before, just as I've never heard so many strange names as I keep hearing in this school. Some kids come all the way from Afghanistan, Somalia, or Peru. I always thought that immigrant kids were unruly, but the white kids in this school are really out of control. They talk back to the teachers—especially Dennis and Jolanda. Teacher Thea introduces me to the class, so luckily, I don't have to say anything. Around me, I hear classmates whispering and making fun of my name. I don't know if I should laugh along or look tough. My face somehow manages a mix of both.

At lunch break, a couple of classmates come to me and say that I need to fight Hannibal. They want me to show that nobody should mess with me. But I'm not bothered by what he said—I don't even know what it means. Half of the time these kids use words I've never heard of. I keep hearing things like "hoe," "yo mama," or even worse, "Your mom's a whore." "Faggot" is common too, but that's no different from Vlissingen. I always freeze when I hear it.

In front of me, I see a few of my classmates pulling Hannibal toward me. It looks like he's resisting, but he can't stop them from dragging him along. When we're face to face, I ask him what he was saying in class. Before he can answer, someone pushes him from behind right toward me. He tries to kick me, but misses. I try to give him a flying kick but miss too. I learned it from one of my favorite movies, *Bloodsport*. After that, we get pulled away from each other. The crowd looks disappointed—they had hoped for a bloody nose at least. On Wednesday, we have Teacher Sally. Teacher Sally is a full-figured woman with black glasses with small round lenses and short, natural, curly hair. She always looks as if she's heading to church after class to sing praises to the Lord and bless His name before catching the Holy Spirit. We start with our weekly hygiene checkup. It's mandatory because we live in a disadvantaged neighborhood, where many kids have tooth decay. At the teacher's orders, everyone stands in a long line, and one by one, we're given a little cup of fluoride to rinse our mouths with. Everyone obeys Teacher Sally without question, more so than any other teacher, so I do the same. Like a sergeant, she walks down the line to inspect our mouths and to check if there's dirt under our fingernails. She stops right next to me in front of Dennis, a real-life version of comic book character Dennis the Menace. I glance quickly at my nails and want to thank Allah on my bare knees that Mom always makes us cut them. Dennis's nails and teeth are very dirty. Apparently not for the first time, because Teacher Sally snaps. It is almost as if the Holy Spirit descended and entered her body in an exceptionally bad mood. She pulls Dennis by his ear to the classroom sink, opens the faucet, and grabs a bar of green soap. She pushes his head under the faucet and sticks the soap in his mouth. He pulls away, gasping for air. Everyone watches in shock, but no one moves. Before he runs out of the classroom and slams the door, he yells things that I've never heard out of an eleven-year-old's mouth before. I try to stop myself, but I can't suppress a smirk, especially because Teacher Sally seems to be praying to purify the classroom from all of the sacrilege from Dennis's mouth.

"If you come into my class like a filthy animal one more time, there'll be hell to pay!"

At the Mercator School, the teachers not only teach, but also check to see if we've had breakfast, if we have any bruises on our bodies, and if we're clean. If a new kid comes in who is behind, I'll be paired with him or her in order to help with math or with Dutch language. Sometimes the pressure is too much for the teachers—I see them pinch, pull hair, and hit kids.

A teacher comes in during class to consult Teacher Thea. At that instance, Dennis cracks me up about something. Again. The teacher looks at me, his face boiling. He walks right up to me.

"Teacher, I wasn't laughing at you."

He pulls me by my collar off of my chair and drags me to the door as if he's taking out the garbage. At the doorway, he grabs my shoulders and kicks me out. I run home crying. Joop is squatting out front, working on his car. Never before have I been so happy to see Joop's butt crack in its full glory greeting me: gravity is really working his jeans. In snot-filled fits and starts, I tell him what happened. He grabs me by the hand and we march to school. His bellowing voice shakes the whole school. Hand in hand, we walk up and down the hallway. He stops in front of every classroom to make sure that everyone can hear him. I hear one "goddammit!" after another. He uses words I don't know in order to make it clear that nobody can ever touch me again. Not a single teacher reacts— they don't even flinch.

Outside the school, on the playground, he transforms back into Joop the teddy bear, just like the Hulk changes into his alter ego Bruce Banner after he calms down. I give him a kiss and head back to class.

Amsterdam is strange. Shawarma is sold everywhere, there are junkies walking around, and I don't understand a lot of phrases, which are spoken in this heavy local accent. If I say "Excuse me?" they look at me like I'm crazy when they're the ones who don't make any sense. Somebody stole a bike from our apartment hallway. In Vlissingen, I could leave my bike unlocked on a different street and it would still be there the next day. Sometimes people would even bring it back to our door themselves. Here, I hear ambulances all day. I hate that sound. But the worst are the letters that I have to read if Ria isn't there. Letters from bill collectors, because something is past due.

The letters sometimes begin with: "In the name of the Queen." I'm so ashamed—even the queen knows that we still haven't paid everything.

Still, I'm starting to warm up to this place more and more. So much so that I've stopped with "Escape from Amsterdam" before bedtime—our secret mission, named after the film *Escape from Alcatraz*. Jamal, Aziz, and Nourdin have also stopped. Usually, we took turns before bed with heartfelt pleas to convince our mom to take us back to Vlissingen. The five of us lay in the only bedroom of our house, each on his own air mattress. It was the happiest moment of the day. We chitchatted until we fell asleep. Every night we thought of new arguments for moving back. Mom never said no—she let us have our silly fantasies, knowing that there was no chance anyway. Now we have beds and no longer whine about moving back to Vlissingen.

Now we whine about new soccer gear, new games for the Super Nintendo, and school supplies. And about designer clothing, especially because I'm about to go to high school. It's just a matter of waiting for the results of the Cito test—the high school admissions exam—and the school's official recommendation. Ria says that I don't need to worry about it. She is keeping track of my report cards and will go to parents' night on Mom's behalf.

The day of the recommendation announcements, the school is a madhouse. Many parents want to talk to someone about their kid's recommendation. They all want the same thing: the highest possible academic track for their kid. I hear teachers complain that they've never seen or talked with many of the immigrant parents who are causing an uproar. When I see my recommendation, I'm stunned: it says I should be on the lower track, despite the fact that my Cito score indicates the highest one. I don't get it. Do they really think that I'm only capable of the lower track? Or do they want to spare me the possible disappointment, in case I can't manage the higher track? The whole year, I've been tutoring other kids at school. I constantly have to wait for new assignments because I finish way before the rest of the students. Teacher Thea praises me all the time because I'm so inquisitive. She says that people who ask a lot of questions become very smart. She praises me in my report card. I have high grades … so what is this all about?

I go to Ria, and she is also surprised. She says that I need to go to school with Mom, but Mom doesn't understand any of this. Just like all of the other parents, she wants me to get into high school in the highest level. Ria comes with us, and we talk with Teacher Thea. We ask her why I got a recommendation for the lower track, despite having good results and always being praised by everyone, including her. She hesitates, leaves to go consult with other teachers, and comes back with good news. I am one of the few students at the school to get a recommendation for the higher track. I'm actually really angry. This isn't right—maybe there were mistakes made with other students too. But I don't want to cause trouble in case they change their minds about me.

On the playground, the father of a Turkish boy in my class comes up to me. He heard that Mom, Ria, and I had a conversation with the teacher. He practically begs me to help him. The look in his eyes is one of pure helplessness. I don't know how I can help him. Ria is already gone, and she was also annoyed that she'd never met many of the angry parents at parents' night. I tell the father that he and his wife need to go and make a fuss with their kid's teacher. The problem is that they barely speak any Dutch. I walk home with an uneasy feeling. Ria is sitting there on a bench in front of their window. I'm so lucky to have her. Mom is sitting next to her, beaming with pride.

Doing the best we can in school is the least we can do for her. She works hard at the snack bar, often until the wee hours of the night, in order to give me and my brothers what we need. It's so unfair. If a Moroccan man gets divorced, he often remarries. That's what Dad did. With Moroccan women, it's different—they stay single. There are many Moroccan single mothers in the neighborhood. Why do they divorce so often? Do they marry too young? Do they want to be free? Why did Mom and Dad really divorce? Sometimes I want to tell Mom that it's okay with me if she follows her heart and finds someone else. I won't get mad. I know for sure that my brothers feel the same way. Sometimes I want to talk about Dad. And on very rare occasions, I wish I could ask about *it*.

But there are some things that we never talk about. You just don't.

4

Either they don't see that I'm sitting there, or they see me and just don't care. It's so weird. If it were any of my brothers or nephews, they would immediately switch into high alert. With me, they don't adjust their body language or censor their conversations. Why do they feel so comfortable around me? They even tell dirty jokes when I'm sitting in their midst, and they hardly look up to see my reaction.

I'm in Morocco, in Khouribga, with my mother's family. I'm sitting in my grandmother's kitchen, along with my aunts and female cousins. This is the first time that I've seen them since Dad passed away, a couple of years ago now. I have many aunts. My grandma only had daughters, and if this shindig in her kitchen were made into a movie, the genre would be drama, action, comedy, romance, and horror wrapped into one. One of them washes a freshly plucked chicken or lets couscous grains slide between her bored fingers, while another makes enormous chunks of sugar disappear into a teeny-tiny teapot or sends one of the boys on an errand. Usually that's my cousin Fouad, who is being raised by my grandma because his mother passed away and his father ran off.

The meal preparations or the day's excessive tea breaks are always accompanied by commentary about the whole neighborhood, especially the women. Whether it's about Khadouj, who was spotted with a brand-new addition to her kitchen, or the wife of the café owner, who is rocking a string of gold bracelets up to her elbow in order to show off to her neighbors, everything is discussed. They shift effortlessly from one household to the other. All of the latest gossip heard at the market or the drugstore is exchanged. They don't spare themselves at all. If one of their sons has been spotted high or drunk, or both, by one of the many spies in their networks, they describe in detail how they'll make him suffer when he comes home. The air is filled with wafting aromas from pots and pans, and hearts opening up.

My aunts look like the women in the photos that I sometimes see in the Netherlands accompanying reports about problems in the Muslim community. Some people would definitely think that they are submissive or subordinate to their husbands. It's too bad that those people can't see what I always see here in my grandma's kitchen. This is the command center, where decisions are made about how to spend the profits from the harvest, who is responsible for what task, and how family crises get resolved.

When they start to whisper, I know they are talking about things that I'm not supposed to hear. Whenever I get nosy and ask what they're talking about, it doesn't take long for me to get all of the juicy details. A lot of times they gossip about trouble in other people's paradise. What they really love to discuss is the latest about which girl has been snatched by a successful Moroccan from abroad. These stories are garnished with my aunts' strategic glances toward their daughters—incentives to also find a rich Moroccan from overseas. Why are they okay with me being among them when they would never allow one of the other boys to sit like this?

I'm relieved when they start with their standard kitchen cross-examination, because it means that they haven't noticed *it*. Even though we've done this so many times, it seems like they can't get enough. Their faces show the same childlike curiosity as the first time. The craziest part is that they aren't acting—they live for this.

"Will you marry a Moroccan or a white woman?"

I don't know, I always say, thankful that they don't seem to suspect *it*.

"Ngel sjitan, djouaz bent bledek li tfahmek ou tfhamha," or "Reject

Satan and marry a woman from your fatherland—someone who understands you, and you her."

I giggle, knowing that they are just warming up and that more questions are coming.

"Will you have the wedding in the Netherlands or in Morocco?"

"I don't know. I want my Dutch friends there, but you too."

Klak, klak, klak—the whole kitchen echoes with the sound. It's the Moroccan equivalent of the Surinamese *tyuri*, a sign of irritation.

"I really want you to be there. It'll work out."

Then they bring out the big guns.

"Are you European or Moroccan?"

"European," my grandma says, having witnessed my birth in Vlissingen. "He was born there, and he lives there." In response, the same aunt always cries, with an imaginary Black Panther fist in the air:

"La, Maghrebi! Matnchas ahlek!"—"No, he is Moroccan! Don't forget your roots!"

This time I'm not sitting with them for the good company. This vacation, I have a mission, and since Dad isn't coming back, my grandma, aunts, and cousins are the only ones who can help me get rid of *it*. I think that I finally know what *it* is and what I need to do. *It* is a "djinn." Djinns are creatures of Allah, just like humans, but they are invisible to the naked eye. They are created out of smokeless fire, the Koran states. Here in Morocco, there are many stories about djinns. They can be good or bad, but most of the stories are scary ones about bad djinns. It's said that people who talk to themselves out loud, who curse for no apparent reason, who are always sad, or who are plagued by strange thoughts are possessed by a djinn. I think strange things. I think that there's a bad one inside of me.

It's just like that girl from *The Exorcist*. That's how *it* feels: like a bad spirit that makes me think forbidden, dirty things and wants to act those things out. I fire one question after another at my grandma, aunts, and cousins about djinns. They spoil me with one story after another, sometimes until the middle of the night. They whisper, sometimes calling out Allah, as if djinns have a special sense that lets them know when they're being talked about. People say that you can be "hit" or "touched" by them if you come in contact with water at night, especially contaminated water. They wander there. Once the djinns are inside you, it is almost impossible to break free from them.

In Vlissingen, I once fell into a ditch. We went to feed ducklings with Dad. I threw breadcrumbs toward them, but I wanted to pet them too. They waddled away, and I ran after them. They jumped into the water, and I fell in, because I didn't see where the grass ended and the water began. Dad grabbed my arm before I fell in completely and fished me out. He was really mad and slapped me afterward. I don't know why, but many Moroccan parents slap their kids instead of hugging them when they get hurt. It must be from the scare, I guess. Then he grabbed newspapers from the trunk and put them on the backseat of the car for me to sit on. Maybe there was a djinn in that ditch, even though it wasn't dark outside.

After lots of prying and asking questions about how to deal with djinns, I finally get an answer from a cousin that I can work with. She says that there is a verse in the Koran that offers protection against djinns. It is "Ayat el Kursi," the "Throne Verse." I write it out in Dutch, and in the evening, I recite the text before I go to sleep. I do this for a week straight, but I don't feel any different. *It* is still there, and it's almost as if I'm thinking about *it* even more. When I continue to bombard my cousin with questions, she directs me to her father, the husband of my mother's oldest sister.

He is a well-known *fkih*. He has studied the Koran and often helps cure people who are dealing with djinns. One time, someone asked him for help late in the evening, when I was sleeping over. It was a hysterical girl from a couple doors up. Shaking, she said that he had to come with her, because a newly born baby had been cursed by a djinn. He grabbed his stuff and hurried over. My cousin and I followed him. Inside, I saw a crying mother with a baby in her arms. The baby had all kinds of bumps on its stomach and could barely breathe. My uncle kneeled next to the woman, sent away the nosy onlookers who had gathered on the street, and, with striking calmness, began reciting verses from the Koran while holding the baby's pinky finger. The last thing I saw, before my cousin pulled me outside too, was how he conjured up a little pot of ink and began to scribble something on a piece of paper.

He's the person I need to talk to—I already knew that—but I don't have the guts. He is used to my endless questions about how heaven and hell look, but he also has knowledge of human nature. He tends to ask many questions in response to mine, and I don't want to risk him catching onto *it*. Who knows if he can sense *it*? But I don't have any other choice—I have to risk it. During the day, when he takes his siesta, I stop by and plop down next to him.

"Gali si el-Arbi, I think there's a djinn inside me."

"Ha ha ha."

"I'm not joking—there's something inside me. I think all kinds of things that I'm not allowed to think."

"Go play outside—kids shouldn't be worrying about djinns."

"Gali . . ."

Okay, that went way differently than I had imagined. I need to think up something else. I don't have much money—just twenty dirhams, about four guilders—but this is well worth it. I go to my aunt and give her ten dirhams. I tell her that I need a piece of paper like the one that my uncle had scribbled on with ink, because I don't feel good. I give her a serious look.

"I've been touched by a djinn."

Her reaction is ambiguous: she laughs, but also shows concern. I beg her not to tell anyone, and she gives me her word. With the other ten dirhams, I go to my cousin, who's gossiping with girls from down the street. As usual, they don't look up, because it's just me. Hopefully that will change soon, and they'll see me the same way they see my brothers and cousins. I want them to chase me out of the kitchen, rather than chatting with me as if I'm one of them.

"Ten dirhams for whoever can tell me how to get rid of a djinn."

What follows is incoherent chatter about *sihr*, or black magic, a big business in Morocco. Remedies for djinns and curses vary, from pricey incantations in which hyenas' brains are used, to cooking dried lizards in the moonlight. I say to the girls that I don't want to do anything that's haram, or forbidden under Islam. I don't want to fight fire with fire. My cousin says that her father uses *el bgor* to purify people of evil influences. I saw him do that once to her sister, who also thought that she was possessed. *El bgor* is a mixture of stones, sticks, and herbs that's laid on burning coals, making fragrant smoke. You have to immerse yourself in the smoke as much as possible in order to heal. They say that it's permitted.

I give them ten dirhams and promise them ten more if they can arrange something for me, but only if this deal stays confidential. I see dollar signs in their eyes, but they tell me I need to wait until tomorrow. Is this what it feels like to win the lottery? When it's time to go to bed, all kinds of thoughts are crossing my head—I can't fall asleep.

I want to be a man, not a sissy. Especially now that Dad is gone. This has to work.

The following afternoon, my aunt gives me a piece of parchment-like paper marked with ink. She says that I need to keep it in my pocket for a couple of weeks. A giggling cousin brings me a small bag with *el bgor*. She also gives me pottery with coals, aluminum foil, and a pack of matches and instructions to ignite all of it. I give her the last ten dirhams I'd promised. She's thrilled, but not as much as I am.

When most of the family is asleep during the daily siesta, I walk to the caves on the edge of town, next to a huge garbage heap. I've been here before to look for scorpions with my brothers, an older cousin, and his friend. There's nobody outside now in this heat, and the scorpions are hidden deep inside the cave where it's coolest. It's not as dark and dangerous at the cave's mouth.

It feels like I'm doing something illegal, as if I could be caught at any moment. But every time I peek outside the cave, I see no sign of life. It's difficult to concentrate on lighting the coals when there are bugs swarming everywhere, trying to crawl under my clothes. The coals are taking their time to burn. I ask Allah for help the whole time. When they are finally burning up, I put the contents of the bag on the foil above the coals. Smoke wafts up, slowly at first, and then more and more. It smells surprisingly nice—I wonder why djinns are afraid of it. Do they hate pleasant scents? I set the bowl on the ground between my legs and stand directly above it. I don't care about the bugs anymore—I've waited so long for this. I absorb the smoke with my body, as if my life depends on it. When the smoke rises more to the left, I move to the left. I don't want to waste any of it. When the smoke decreases, I light the remaining coals and start again. I'm holding the piece of paper in my hand, pressed against my chest. When all the coals turn to ash, it's over. This will have to do.

Back in Amsterdam, it's the start of high school—I attend the Reformed Lyceum West. It's the only high school with the higher academic track in Amsterdam-West. I'm in a mixed freshman class. It's not long before I fall in love for the first time in my life. With Veena, the prettiest girl in school. I think the magical cave worked.

The djinn has been dispelled.

5

"Mohammed, why do you drink?"

Mohammed rolls his eyes.

"Mohammed, why do you drink? You know it's not allowed."

"This again?"

"Why can't you just drink Fanta like us?"

Mohammed, Sufian, and I are all students at the Reformed Lyceum West and have become best friends. All three of us are Muslim, each in his own way. I've been terrorizing Mohammed for a while because he's experimenting with alcohol and pot. Alcohol is haram, and pot too. I don't understand why he doesn't care. A while ago he was seriously contemplating whether Allah really exists. As if that wasn't enough, he wore silver pants the last time we went to Paradiso, a popular club. We call him "Spaceman," after that song by Babylon Zoo, where the singer in the video wears silver pants. I also heard that Hassan, a cool kid in school, doesn't fast during Ramadan. I really don't get it. What would *they* say about them?

Don't they care about that? I sure do. I'm still afraid of the djinn coming back. Sometimes I feel *it* slumbering, but is it really a djinn? I'm not so sure anymore. Maybe it's just something I was born with— something from Allah? If that's so, why was I in love with Veena, even though she didn't feel the same way? Why do I look at girls? I just saw another cute girl at Paradiso—Moluccan, I think—and I hope she'll be there next time.

Paradiso is the only club where they don't play only Top 40 music or trance and we don't get turned away at the door. Waiting in line is still stressful because of that one humiliating incident, which I feel anew every time we go out. The first time I went out, I went to Rembrandt Square with the coolest crowd from school. My hair, outfit, and Timberlands were fresh—I was feeling myself. We could hear the music from outside. Everyone in the long line was bumping their head to the beat, except for me. I was a nervous wreck because of all of the stories I'd heard. I tried to act as normal as possible and gave my friendliest look to the bouncer, a big, bald white guy in his forties. Just before I got to the front of the line, he pointed at me, devoid of emotion. He plucked me like a rotten apple out of a basket.

"Sorry man, you're not coming in. Move along."

I tried to jump out of the line as fast as possible, hoping that no one saw, but everyone from school was looking. They felt sorry for me, but they went in anyway. No one said anything, and I didn't either. I almost wanted to stay home sick that Monday, but then everyone would know how hurt I was. Did he turn me away because I'm Moroccan? What other reason could there be? I'm pretty small, so maybe he thought that I was too young? I had my ID with me, so he could have asked how old I was.

Everyone in the neighborhood complains about being turned away at clubs. At school that Monday, someone said that the club had a Black bartender, so they couldn't possibly be racist. And Jessie, who's Indonesian, got in.

I love Paradiso, not only because of the inclusive door policy and the mixed crowd, but especially because of the music. Especially the "Paradisco," where they spin classics from the '80s, and the "Bassline," where they blast R&B and hip-hop, are dope. Ever since I heard Puff Daddy and Mase's "Can't Nobody Hold Me Down," I've been listening to this style of music day and night and practice their steps in front of the mirror. I study the lyrics more closely than I do my schoolbooks, and my friends and I always discuss who the best R&B singers and hip-hop lyricists are, at school and on the street. In some songs I hear "faggot," including those of my favorite rappers—Nas in "Halftime," Jay-Z in "22 Two's," Biggie in "The What." They use it as a slur for men who don't act like real men. Whenever I hear the word—at school, on the block, in movies, in music—*it* is a slur. Everyone thinks *it* is bad.

I just need to pray, and then *it* will stay away. We were never forced to pray at home—our parents left it up to us. I'll ask Sufian. I go to his house a lot because we both collect comics. Together with his sisters Jihad, Hajar, and Esmaa, they teach me how to pray and how the *wudu* goes—the purification ritual before prayer. It's way easier than I thought, so I don't have an excuse anymore. I don't want to keep saying to that group of nosy mosque-goers that walks by while we're playing tennis that I don't pray. Sufian does pray, and he goes to the mosque with his father. What will *they* think of me? I don't want *them* to think that I'm not a real Muslim. I am.

I like going out a lot more than I like praying. *They* say that going out is forbidden because alcohol is served. But Sufian and other kids from school who pray go out too. I don't know—*they* say so many things that it sometimes drives me crazy. Say what you want about Mohammed—at least he isn't afraid to ask questions. He is actually educating himself on what he believes and why. Some kids from school and my neighborhood only go to the mosque because their fathers make them. Their fathers just want them to go because they're imitating other fathers. Or am I only fooling myself because I'm not doing what a true Muslim should be doing?

Sometimes this religion feels like an heirloom, something passed down from generation to generation. I got it from my mother and father, they got it from my grandmother and grandfather, and so on: no questions asked. Sufian's father, who knows a lot about Islam, once said that the first word in the Koran is *iqra*: read. "Read" sounds like an instruction, like homework, but out of all the Muslims I know, who has actually read it for themselves? Most of them only know a few popular verses, like I do. Most of our understanding of Islam comes from religious scholars, who have studied the Arabic in which the

Koran is written. Who knows if they got it right? If I blindly follow a scholar's explanation, simply because everyone else does, without doing any research myself, who am I really worshiping?

That's why I hated the Koran lessons in Vlissingen, even though we didn't have to take them for long. The only thing we did there was memorize lines and recite verses. We never actually discussed the deeper meaning of the words. Fortunately, my father rescued my brothers and me from that sadistic teacher when we told him that he hit our fingertips with a thin reed whenever he felt like it.

Mohammed, by contrast, is doing the right thing, asking questions. He's proving that he cares, that his faith is not an heirloom, but something he's choosing himself. He is doing what I'm afraid to do—what almost no one I know is doing. It's always: "But my father says that it's this way," or "If the imam says it, who are we to say otherwise?" or "The second cousin of the friend of what's-his-name's wife knows a lot, and he says . . ." or "You're not really going to contradict the scholars, right?"

I want to ask someone what the Koran says about *it*, and why *they* say that *it* is forbidden. I hold back, because I'm afraid that someone will become suspicious. The last person who made a comment was one of the mosque-goers who walks up to us every once in a while by the tennis courts in the Bos en Lommer neighborhood. We play tennis there almost every day, even if it's raining. We recognize them from far away because they wear white robes and just-trimmed beards. They never give up: today, with renewed energy, they make the umpteenth pitch to lure us to the mosque. This time, they don't use a vivid description of hell, but rather the warning that the day of judgment is approaching. One of the signs of the end of our existence, according to one of them, is "men in dresses." He means drag queens.

When we're not in school, playing tennis, or going out, I go to Henk, a comics store in the center of the city. The shop belongs to Henk, who looks like anything but a Henk. He is a Chinese nerd with a beer belly who sells American comics that you can hardly find anywhere else. There's no better feeling in the world than picking up a fresh stack of X-Men comics, rushing home, and spending the whole day reading in my room. Henk is tucked away on the Zeedijk, between a bunch of small Chinese businesses, pot-selling "coffee shops," and sex shops. In order to get to Henk, I have to pass the prostitutes in the red-light district. I walk quickly so that no one sees me here—you never know what *they* will think. When I peep at the red-lit windows, I sometimes see Moroccan and Turkish men standing among the tourists.

I love the X-Men so much because they show what it's like to be a minority in society. The X-Men are people who are born with an X-gene, which makes them different. That being-different means they are seen by the establishment as a threat to stability. They have one adventure after another with their superpowers, but underneath all of the adventure is a story of how to deal with being feared and hated when you're different. The hatred for mutants in the X-Men is a metaphor for the hate in our world for women and ethnic and sexual minorities. I recognize stuff from my own life, like being turned away at the club, or when a group of us are profiled by the police for no reason. I learn a lot from the way the X-Men deal with being seen as "the other": "Sworn to protect a world that hates and fears them." When I disappear into a comic and resurface after I'm finished, it feels like I can deal with stuff more easily, like that time with that old guy on August Allebé Square.

I'm grocery shopping at Albert Heijn and run into a couple of friends. As usual, we talk about going out. An old bald man with a cranky face is sitting on a bench next to us, watching. I can see him listening, but he probably won't understand much. We're switching back and forth between Dutch and Moroccan, with a Surinamese word here, a Turkish expression or American slang there. This must sound alien to his ears. It's not long before he completely loses it.

"When are you going to leave this place? When will you just go? Everyone left except for you!"

We're shocked, wondering if we should say something, but we can't find the words. I think we all understand what he's trying to say. His old neighborhood is gone. If I had superpowers and could hover right over the square and look below, I would see him literally surrounded by a mosque, a Turkish grocer, a Moroccan café, and people who don't look like him and with whom he can't even have a simple conversation. For him, we're mutants, X-Men of sorts. He's not a racist, and we're not guilty of anything, but still, something is off here.

It's crowded inside me: the Netherlands, Morocco, Islam, *it*, and *them*. They're elbowing each other, stepping on each other's feet, pointing the finger at each other. It's hard to keep them away from each other or to bring them together.

Comics are like a gift from heaven, but however real their stories about good and evil may seem, it's still men and women in spandex talking to each other in speech balloons. No one I know or see is like me. On TV and in movies, it's always Ross and Rachel. If I ever see *it*, he doesn't look like me, and there's something scary happening, like with Tom Hanks in *Philadelphia*. Or it's the flamboyant type, like Elton John. I just want to meet someone like me for a change. Do they even exist? I'm so curious about what their life looks like.

I'm on my way to Henk to pick up a new stack of comics. It's Ramadan. An old, bald Moroccan man walks in front of me, clearly in a hurry, probably also trying to buy something before sundown. He stops in front of the McDonald's on Leidsestraat. He stares inside. Two Moroccan girls are sitting there, chatting and eating. He makes a scene: how dare they not fast, what would their parents say if they knew that they were sitting here during Ramadan, what wrath they will face in the afterlife, and so on. Tourists start to gather around him.

Inside, a tug-of-war starts between the girls: one wants to curse him out, while the other wants her to just keep quiet. The furious one wins, storms outside, and yells, with one hand on her hip and one in the air: "We're on our periods!"

The man's mouth falls so far open that a Big Mac could fit in easily. Women on their periods are exempt from fasting. With his head lowered, his tail between his legs, and his face as red as the McDonald's logo, he takes off. It's only fifteen minutes from the square where the cranky old man sat to this McDonald's, yet it's like I'm traveling from one planet to another on a spaceship.

I really need to stop terrorizing Mohammed. I need to stop saying things like "Look, look, she's wearing a headscarf, but her ass is showing in those pants." I need to stop gossiping about who was supposedly caught eating pork or secretly didn't observe Ramadan. My father also did things that aren't allowed. Sometimes I saw beer bottles hidden in the fridge. He had a tattoo. *They* say that tattoos are haram, because they permanently alter Allah's creation. If that's true, is my father not in heaven? People aren't allowed to play Allah, yet all of the Muslims I know behave like bouncers at the gates of heaven, without having an entry ticket themselves.

At school, discussions about what's haram and what isn't migrate from the theology or social studies class to the hallway, from the hallway to the cafeteria, and from the cafeteria to the playground. The Barcelona-versus-Real-Madrid equivalent of these discussions always comes down to sex and love. Most of the time, it's the boys against the girls.

"So *you* can have sex before marriage because you're boys, and we can't?"

"It's different for women."

"Isn't premarital sex haram for everyone?"

"Yes, but don't you want a man who knows what he's doing?"

"Hypocrites—you want to marry virgins, but you can fuck whoever you want."

In my heart, I choose the girls' side, but on the outside, I stay quiet. I don't want to trigger anyone into asking me questions about my love life, because before you know it, they'll see something on my face or detect something in my voice. I've become an expert at camouflaging myself in these types of situations. That's why, when Street Fighter II came out on the Super Nintendo, I never played with Chun-Li if someone else was around. She was my favorite character, and I almost always won with her, but all the other boys played with male characters. So I chose Vega or Dhalsim instead.

We never discuss *it*, as if everyone agrees that that's really next-level haram. If there is a hierarchy of what's haram, I'd be on top. That's why I'm so eager to condemn Mohammed and others. It's not that I want them to act like angels. I want them to sin as much as possible—the more the better. Maybe if all of their sins are combined, they'll be as nasty as my sin. If everyone has an *it*, then no one can play Allah but Allah Himself.

6

Growing up, when one of my brothers broke something in the house, we would all get punished, not just the culprit. We'd wait with nail-biting dread for our parents to come home. As soon as I heard the key in the front door, I'd run quick as an arrow to the farthest corner of the couch and sit all puppy-eyed. Before my mother—who can spot microscopic little stains in the most obscure places—found the scene of the crime and went looking for a sandal to use for a collective beating, I tried to talk my way out of it.

"I swear, it wasn't me."

I sit with my mother in the living room when we see how two glorious skyscrapers in New York are destroyed by two airplanes hijacked by extremist Muslims. When I see my mother's reaction, it's like I've stepped into a time machine and am sitting on the couch again, staring at the front door, hoping they will see that I had nothing to do with it and spare me the sandal. Whatever I said or did, the sandal didn't differentiate between my brothers and me. The more I see and hear—the people falling from the towers, the final phone conversations with loved ones—the more I feel as if I have something to explain. I try to act nonchalant in front of my panicking mother, but my jaw won't relax.

The terrorist attack coincides with me preparing to spend a few months in New York at the beginning of the next year. Now that Jamal is a professional soccer player and has a contract with AZ Alkmaar, with a huge salary, I don't have to stress about leaving my family behind. I've saved some of my pay from soul-killing telemarketing jobs, and I'm sure my brother will help me out as well. This is a chance to figure out what I want to do with my life, far from all of the responsibilities, far from *them*. I'm almost twenty-one and don't even know what I want to study. The year I spent studying criminology at the Vrije Universiteit Amsterdam definitely was not what I wanted, even though I don't have a clue what I actually want. Aside from some messing around with girls, I still haven't had a serious relationship. I dream of drawing comics for Marvel and making movies. Marvel is based in New York, and there are renowned film schools there. It's the best place to get a clear head and figure out which way to go in life.

My mother is worried about how *el Hollandiyin*, the Dutch, will react to us after 9/11. She says it's dumb that we never registered for our Moroccan passports. Our Moroccan neighbor, who always chats with me when I run into him on the stairs—often giving me a dramatic motivational speech about doing my best in school—advises me, while holding my arm, that "we" need to stay calm. "Show yourself in the best light," says the owner of a Moroccan food stall in the neighborhood when I order a hot chicken sandwich and an avocado shake. Maybe I'm imagining this, but it's almost like the first generation of Moroccan immigrants in the neighborhood are walking around with a bent back because of invisible suitcases—as if they're thinking of an emergency exit to Morocco if shit hits the fan.

The *Hollandiyin*, especially the older generation, aren't holding back on their feelings wherever I go. It reminds me of the time I worked at Interview-NSS and we were doing phone surveys about quality of life in different areas in the city. Since people would often hang up or ask questions about the roots of my name, I renamed myself "Jeremiah Meijer." This alias had an amazing effect on the number of surveys I was able to complete. A lot fewer people hung up on me. One time I got an old woman on the line and asked her the standard boring questions about her street and her apartment, how clean and safe it was, and so on. Compared to other people I spoke to, her answers were, to put it mildly, unusual. Without hesitation, she cut loose about the doorway that is always blocked by "fat women with headscarves who reek of BO" and about "unassimilated immigrants" everyone hated and how something really needed to be done to get rid of them. She demanded that I write everything down word for word, which I did. After the conversation, I gave her number to some of the coworkers in my row. We often did that with nasty respondents. They took turns calling her with heavy, fake accents and made-up Moroccan names until she got so irritated that she disconnected her phone.

Every day on TV, I see one Muslim after another making a plea "not to paint everyone with a single brush" and emphasize that "other religions have extremists too," but they fall on deaf ears and the "Yes, but …"

"Yes, but it says here that you're allowed to hit women."

"Yes, but what do you all think of gays?"

"Yes, but you consider Jews and atheists to be inferior."

The only thing I can think of to do against all this ignorance is to participate in the discussions on www.fok.nl, a popular online youth forum. A lot of white people don't know any Muslims and have little insight into how we live. Who knows … maybe by explaining my religion and talking with people, I can convince them that there's no hidden Muslim agenda for Islamic world domination or the oppression of non-Muslims. In my free time, at an internet café on Kinkerstraat near our apartment, I search for information to use in my debates with people online who say that Islam is not only inherently bad, but also worse than all other religions. I look up statistics, read about extremism in other religions, and delve into a new topic about Muslims every day. There are plenty of topics to keep me busy. To my surprise, I'm bombarded by non-Muslims with Koran verses and quotes from hadith—accounts of the life of the prophet Mohammed.

As if it isn't already stressful enough to be a Muslim dealing with the judgmental eyes and sharp tongues of fellow Muslims, you now have to deal with hordes of non-Muslims as well. Quoting out of context and copying whatever Google produces, they pretend they're Allah and know what a "real" Muslim should be like. It makes me think of how everyone in elementary school sang along with 2 Unlimited's "No Limit" and Ace of Base's "All That She Wants" without knowing the exact words. It was all about the experience of producing sounds. Still, I'm eager to find the right context and accurate translation so that I understand it myself. I can't remember being this preoccupied with my religion when I was in high school. Sometimes I sit until after midnight, with four empty Coke bottles next to the screen, typing like crazy, eyes strained from the light. We discuss everything, from the oft-quoted verses about Christians and Jews and about women and gay people, to the question of whether dogs are allowed and if Muslims can listen to music. It's one big ping-pong game: a citation from the Koran or hadith comes up, and immediately I reply with my interpretation of it. The next day I can't wait to log on again and see where the discussion is heading.

I'm a lot less eager to join any discussion about the story of the prophet Lot—the Islamic version of the Bible's Sodom and Gomorrah. In many Islamic countries, this story is used as the basis for the ban on homosexuality, with prosecution and sometimes even the death penalty as punishment. Usually within Islam, you can find all kinds of alternative readings of the verses that showcase diversity in religious interpretations. But I don't see them with this subject, although I never really dare to dive into them. It's as if everyone in the Muslim community agrees that *it* is wrong. Not even the website submission.org, where my friend Emre and I got a lot of inspiration from other thorough, original interpretations, offers an opening. *It* hurts. Not because it puts me in a weaker position in online discussions, but because I hope that *they* got it all wrong, that *they* missed something.

When I'm not knee-deep in a theological discussion, I google to try and discover cool things to do in New York. I'm almost leaving. Through a spontaneous series of clicks, I stumble on *Paris Is Burning*, a documentary by Jennie Livingston about the so-called ball scene in 1980s New York. The ball scene is made up of parties where ethnic minorities who have *it* come together to act out their fantasies, with extravagant outfits and accessories. There are different "houses," each with different members, which compete against each other for a prize. Every house has a "mother" at its head. The houses serve as a metaphor for the new families that are forged by these outsiders. In the competition, the participants make their mothers proud by winning trophies, and the house with the most trophies gets the highest status.

A ball is the very word. Whatever you want to be, you be. [...] You can become anything and do anything, right here right now, and won't be questioned.

That's what I long for: not to be plagued anymore by the same questions over and over. The Black and Latino boys often hang around the area by the Christopher Street Pier. Some look for a place to sleep there because they've been disowned by their families; others pick up clients who pay for sex; most look for kindred spirits. When I get to New York, the first thing I'm gonna do is visit the Christopher Street Pier.

The day of my literal and figurative flight is emotional. My mother is overdoing the crying part, almost as if she'll never see me again. Mothers sense certain things, and it wouldn't surprise me if she has known all along why I have to do this. She never really tried to stop me—maybe she really knows why I want to go so badly? I say goodbye to my brothers and friends and go to Schiphol Airport, where I'm subjected to an endless circus of questions because of new rules since 9/11. The young man in uniform standing at some kind of interrogation booth wants to know what I do in my daily life, where I'll be staying, who I know there, why I have a one-way ticket instead of roundtrip, whether I'm a believer, how much I practice my religion, what I think about New York, and more. I'm so excited about this trip that I can't help but enjoy answering all of the questions in detail, and by the look on his disciplined, professional face, he seems to notice.

In the waiting area at the gate, I see an Arab man dressed in a three-piece suit with a leather suitcase in his hand. He has a neatly groomed, pitch-black beard. It's crowded, but the seat next to him is empty. I try not to stare, but I can't help it. I'm not the only one. He is sitting undisturbed, gazing out as if all of the staring and whispering don't faze him at all. I catch myself hoping he was checked even more thoroughly by security than I've been. For a moment, the adrenaline that the prospect of New York unleashes in me is completely overshadowed by a sense of doom that this man makes me feel. If a majority of the people in the waiting area had the power, wouldn't they probably have him subjected to a different security check than us, or even not allowed him on the plane? Would I rather not have him on board?

On the airplane, I sit next to a chubby American who had been in the Netherlands on business. He asks if I'm Muslim and how I feel, with everything that's happening. He says he was nervous about the man with the beard. I confess that I felt a bit nervous too.

"Really?"

I nod, embarrassed.

"To be honest, I was a little nervous about you as well."

I didn't see that coming.

"I guess it sucks to be a Muslim right now."

"I guess."

7

Human crowds zigzag out of all kinds of openings in the ground, as if Allah is poking an anthill with an invisible stick. High in the air, giant billboards compete for attention with their most original pick-up lines. Everywhere, seas of flowers are illuminated by burning candles: the streets, wounded by terrorists, are stitched up with shrines for heroic firemen. My senses do somersaults and backflips as I turn around. I taste with my nose, smell with my eyes, watch with my ears. The glaring neon lights, penetrating smells, and bombastic sounds lure me into streets and avenues like a kid in a candy store. My feet hurt like hell from walking, but my mind is in heaven. In Amsterdam, I wander around like I'm Kevin in *Home Alone 2*, but in New York, it's more like Dorothy in *The Wizard of Oz*.

When it's almost evening, it's time for a scene that played out in my mind nonstop on the flight from Amsterdam. I only have to muster up enough courage first. I've seen it in so many movies—it's not that complicated. I walk to the sidewalk, step carefully to the edge of the street, and look left and right. There's one. Okay, deep breath, don't worry. I've rehearsed—I know my script. Hand in the air.

"Taxi!"

He's stopping!

"Where we going to?"

I try to suppress a nervous laugh and say: "Christopher ha ha ha ha Street Pier, please."

"Somebody is happy today."

The trail of yellow taxis coloring the street is like the yellow brick road, a road to a magical place that may or may not exist. He drops me off a couple of minutes from the pier, on Christopher Street. I walk past a Chinese nail salon, a fortune-teller, and all kinds of bars with waving rainbow flags at their doors. I stop at some stairs with a view of the pier. I move some empty packaging, beer bottles, and a broken wine bottle to the side and sit on the top step. Like an owl, I scan all of the passersby from a safe distance.

Groups of two or three guys my age and younger walk up and down the street wearing oversized shirts and wide, sagging pants, with boxer shorts underneath constantly playing "peek-a-boo." Their backpacks hang loosely from their elbows. They stop on the pier and walk back again. I see some of them walk back and forth ten times. They don't go into the different bars or food joints. I see cars in the street following the same pattern: they come and go, always the same ones. Now and then one of the guys walks up to a car; the window rolls down, and a short conversation takes place. When a young Latino guy gets into a big black car, I see one of the two Black guys who stay behind read the license plate number aloud while the other saves it in his phone. The Latinos look a lot like Moroccan-Dutch people. I walk toward the pier and check out the scenery some more. There are almost only African American guys and girls. They're drinking and smoking pot, and some of them are sleeping on pieces of cardboard. It reminds me of what a guy in the beginning of *Paris Is Burning* said.

I remember my dad used to say, you have three strikes against you in this world. Every Black man has two, that they're just Black and they're male. But you're Black and you're male and you're gay. You're gonna have a hard fucking time. And he said, if you're gonna do this, you're gonna have to be stronger than you ever imagined.

One of the bars I walk by, the Hangar, looks okay, but I've never been in a bar by myself, let alone this kind of bar. If I think about it too long, I'll chicken out, so I switch my brain off for a second and walk right in. Next to the door is a big window that passersby can easily look through. I spend a couple minutes figuring out where to sit until I find a seat at the bar next to a pool table, which feels safe enough. You never know who might come by.

There are mostly Latino and Black men inside, young and old. The rather heavyset white bartender asks what I want to drink. "Do you have something fruity?" He cracks up. "Fruity? Honey, everything here is fruity!" I don't get the joke, but I laugh along. A huge glass with a peach-colored drink lands in front of me, with colored straws and an umbrella. I've tried a few sips of alcohol a couple of times before, but this is the first time I'm gonna have a full drink.

"So where you from?" begins an animated conversation with the bartender. I tell him that this is the first time I've been on my own, and I'm trying to learn more about myself. He tells me how he moved from the South to New York long ago for a similar reason. I don't know if it's because of this "fruity" liquid or something else, but I keep wanting to thank him the whole time. This is the first time in my life that I'm talking so openly and honestly with someone about *it*. He talks about things that everyone talks about—normal stuff. Whenever he's not paying attention, I check him out from top to bottom. He's no unicorn and has no glittery tail—he's just normal. Why did I expect something else?

"Are you checking me out?"

I laugh and say: "I've never spoken to someone like you."

"So?"

"You're so normal."

"Normal? That's the biggest insult I've ever gotten!"

It's all just like in Oz. The bartender is no magician—just a regular guy. Life's not one big party for the young people on the pier. It's tough, but they make the best of it. That's what's so magical about it. If this were some sort of utopia, I would have stressed all these years for no reason. Now *that* would be disillusioning. I still don't know if it's from the drink or something else, but before I leave, I hug and thank the bartender.

"Honey, bartenders are like shrinks: you pay us, and we give you something to ease your mind."

On the way home, I come across a deli with a buffet full of kosher meat. I order some food to go and catch the subway to Canal Street. I found a cheap room with a Turkish couple in Chinatown, close to the subway station. As soon as I come inside, I use the bed to spread out the promo flyers that I got from the bartender for all of these exciting parties. Before I drift off to dreamland, I hide them in the bottom of my suitcase. You never know who might be snooping around.

The next couple of days, I wander around the city. I feed peanuts to the cheeky squirrels in Central Park, buy bootleg CDs in Brooklyn, and ride the subway, criss-crossing different neighborhoods that I used to visualize, listening to songs by KRS-One, Mobb Deep, and Big L. When the weekend arrives, I grab one of the flyers, which has become crumpled from all of the times I've looked at it. This looks like a really cool party—hip-hop and R&B in Queens, with a mixed crowd.

At night, my stomach starts acting weirdly, just like when you look down from the highest point on a roller coaster before diving to earth. I get myself ready as if it's school picture day: the floor of my room is covered with clothes, and I fight for hours with rebellious hairs that refuse to obey my vanity. The Turkish couple is peeping at me as I walk in and out of the bathroom.

I end up wearing the outfit that I'd tried on first: light-colored Dolce & Gabbana jeans and a light-yellow Diesel shirt.

"You gonna party?"

Shit! What should I say if they ask where I'm going?

"Yes."

"What party?"

"I don't know yet.... I never went out by myself before, I think I'm just gonna go with the flow. You wanna come?"

Why? Why did I do that? Now they might want to come along.

"No, thank you. We're staying in tonight ... busy day tomorrow."

They suggest a few bars before I go out the door. As if there's any chance that I'm going anywhere other than Queens. I catch the subway. It's quite far, but I'm pretty sure that the club is right around the corner from the station. When I walk out of the station, I see a long line in front of the entrance, with Krash lit up above. I look at the people in line and look at the flyer again just to be sure that this is really the right address. It says Krash. This is it, but I can't believe my eyes. The people in the line ... it's like I'm looking at characters from *Boyz n the Hood* and *Blood In, Blood Out*. I can't imagine that they touch each other in that way. I don't get it. You'd never think *it* of them.

Why hasn't anyone ever told me this?

With every step closer to the door I ask myself if I'm about to walk into heaven or hell. Before I show my ID and walk in, I turn to look behind me one more time.

Act normal. No one knows you here.

I head directly to the bar when I get inside. I order a screwdriver and look for an empty spot on the edge of the dance floor. Like at the Hangar, the glass is gigantic: even after ten sips, followed by ten sour expressions, it still looks completely full.

Then, out of nowhere, someone pinches my butt. I turn around but see no one. I was known for doing the same thing to girls back in school. That must have been so annoying.

I go stand on the other side of the dance floor. Whenever someone catches my eye, I look away—otherwise they'll think I want something. One guy comes up to me—a Latino with a flashy necklace, white tank top, yellow Timberlands, and wide, slightly saggy jeans. He looks like he popped right out of a slick Hype Williams video.

"What's going on?"

Astagfirullah, I think as hard as I can, asking for forgiveness for all of the filthy thoughts that come tumbling through my mind.

"I'm good."

He keeps talking, but after a short tug-of-war between the angel and the devil on my shoulders, I walk away, although I give the angel a side-eye. Just as I'm wondering if I should take a taxi home, I hear that unmistakable Timbaland beat. I don't know if it's a sign from above, but the DJ spins "Oops (Oh My)" by Tweet. *I tried and I tried to avoid but this thing was happening, swallowed my pride, let it ride and partied.* After that Mary J. takes it up a notch with *Let loose and set your body free.*

I take a couple of big sips, order another drink, and slowly start to move and groove. After a while, a light-skinned girl grabs my hand just like that. I'm feeling the alcohol, because without hesitating, I go right along. We bump and grind to one R&B and hip-hop hit after another, until a guy comes along—a young Black guy with cornrows, a black T-shirt, baggy jeans, and tattoos. At first, I think that he's with her, but he's looking in my direction.

Astagfirullah.

He keeps looking, and I look back.

Astagfirullah.

He comes closer. The girl takes off, as if she knows what's going to happen. I feel guilty, but she doesn't seem to care. I don't know what to do. For a minute, I even think about running outside. More eye contact. I don't want to go home, but this isn't allowed.

Ya rabbi, if this is wrong, send a meteor to strike me down right now.

He's standing right in front of me—no meteor. We touch each other, and still nothing. Where is that meteor?

The most secret of my secret wishes is happening right now.

I turn my face away. *They* flash by, carried by the lights of the club: my brothers, who'll be ashamed by what others will say; my favorite MCs, who spit "faggot" into the mic; an old classmate, who is now very religious; my aunts, who are looking forward to my wedding in Morocco—I hear *them* through the speakers.

He asks if I want to go sit with him in a quieter lounge area at the back of the club. His name is Eric, and he works at a community center with disadvantaged youth. He tries to kiss me again, but I pull back.

"I'm sorry if I led you on—this is the first time I did something like this with someone like you...."

He smiles and says it's okay. "Can I have your number? I would love to see you another time."

I give him my number and take a taxi to Chinatown. Before I go to sleep, I always do the *shahada*, but now I'm not so sure. How can I call on Allah, after everything I just did?

The following day, Eric calls to ask if I want to get a drink and a bite to eat with him. He picks me up in his brother's black Hummer. We eat Chinese, and I meet his friends: Ty, a shy, mixed-race dancer, and Cindy, a Puerto Rican who—from what I'm overhearing her say over the phone—has both a boyfriend and a girlfriend, as well as a Yorkshire terrier. She asks me if I'm Puerto Rican too. Eric organizes all kinds of activities for youth, from tutoring and job application support to basketball tournaments. We talk for hours about what *it* is—it's all familiar. From this night on, we are inseparable. He takes me to his job, we go to movies, we give out condoms at popular spots. He even takes me to his mother's house one night, where his family is having some kind of an intervention for his addicted sister. The days, weeks, and months fly by, one unbelievable moment after the other.

I have to move out from my room in Chinatown, because my time there is up. I see an ad in the *Village Voice* for a room in Harlem, in an apartment tower next to a busy basketball court. The room is twice as big as the old one, and the owner, an African American woman around thirty, seems cool. I take the room. Lucky me, there's a stereo. The bootleg CDs that I bought don't make a sound, so I have to work with the two CDs that I brought from home: *Illmatic*, by Nas, and *Butterfly*, by Mariah Carey. From my room, I have a view of the basketball court and the parking lot where Eric picks me up.

Today I'm going to an after-party for the first time. I didn't know that such a thing existed, but apparently when the regular clubs close, there are other clubs that stay open until morning, or even until the afternoon. First, we all drive to a diner to eat something, and then straight to Hell's Kitchen, where Club Exit is. It's big, with multiple floors. The laser show is mesmerizing—even if you're sober. Eric, Ty, and Cindy are going to take "E." I've noticed for a while that Eric and his friends sell drugs to their acquaintances. It helps them pay their bills. As long as they leave me out of it, I don't have a problem with it. They ask if I want some too. I'm still not fond of people who can only have fun with alcohol or drugs, but I'm so curious about how it feels. They ask me to go with them to the bathroom—Cindy to the women's, we to the men's. There's a long line. Everyone has a water bottle with them, and there are a bunch of people coming out of one stall at the same time. Weird. Eric and Ty also go into a stall and pull me along. Before I know it, Eric conjures up a bag, pulls out some pills, and washes one down with a sip of water. Ty does the same. They say that I need to decide fast—we can't stay in the bathroom long.

"If you're scared, take half."

I take half a pill, drink a couple sips of water, and go out on the dance floor. For like half an hour, I don't feel anything. Maybe half a pill doesn't do anything? "Do you feel anything? I don't feel anything," I ask every few minutes, until I start to feel a tingling. It turns into goose bumps over my whole body, and my hands feel different. The laser show is hypnotizing me. I follow the lights as they travel from one corner of the room to the other. When I look at the time, I see that I've only been standing here for a couple of minutes, but it feels like an hour. I say "Hi" to everyone whose eyes meet mine. An older blonde woman in a bra—she has taken off her white blouse—greets me by giving me a big hug and kisses on my neck. A really tall man dressed as a woman asks me where I'm from and if I'm enjoying myself. Everyone is so friendly.

Eric and Cindy disappear with people every once in a while, maybe to sell them pills. Why have I never done this before? It's amazing.

Huh?

Everything is normal again. The feeling is gone.

Has the pill already worn off? Why did I only take half anyway? Should I ask Eric for more?

I don't see him, but I do see the beefy guy who asked me if I needed something when I came out of the bathroom. I think he sells too. He's dancing right in front of me. I can just ask him.

"Do you have some E?"

He walks with me to a dark corner of the room and gives me a whole pill—for free.

"Thank you so much."

I've lost Eric, Ty, and Cindy. I try to get into the music again and hear an angry woman's voice. I don't know who it is, but the lyrics feel like they're blasting through speakers inside my skull.

Fire, fire . . .

Here's a lesson, you will learn . . .

Play with fire, you'll get burned.

I'm playing with fire—talking with "men in dresses," taking drugs. The lasers aren't dancing through the room anymore, but attacking me instead. I take a sip of water, but with each sip I want more. I can refill my bottle in the bathroom—everyone does that. I drink the whole bottle and fill it up again. Big eyes and clenched jaws are circling around me. I look in the mirror.

Jesus.

I look like a monster. My heart is beating faster and faster. This is how dying feels. I need more water, and I need to find Eric. When I leave the bathroom, I see him and Ty. I say that I can't stop drinking water, and he grabs the bottle out of my hand right away. They take me up to the top floor, where there's a lounge area with couches. Ty grabs candy, because sugar helps. He says that I need to take off my socks and shoes. He's right. When my feet hit the floor, it feels like I'm coming back down. They say that everyone experiences this sometimes—it's called a bad trip. I go with them to the apartment where Eric and Cindy live.

The next day, they make soup for me, and we talk about all of the bad trips they've had. It takes a few weeks before I begin to feel like I'm somewhat back to normal, but something is still off. Driving around from club to club is beginning to feel shallow. Eric's eyes begin to wander because I don't want to have sex with him. Every time I get a phone call from back home, I'm starting to wonder what I'm doing here. They ask me what's going on with studying and drawing, but I'm not doing any of that.

The distance from *them* hasn't changed how I feel about *it* at all. I ask Eric, who knows a lot about house music, if he knows that song that's been playing in my head since that night. It's "Fire," by Dolce. It wouldn't surprise me if the bad trip was my punishment for playing with fire, because that's what I'm doing here. It's a sign that I need to go home.

8

They have no names and no faces. But when it gets dark, they're here, just like me—the djinns in the chat room. Are they sitting in internet cafés too? Maybe there's even one here. I try to stay away from them, but it's hard. They know how *it* is, even more than in New York, because they're more like me in many ways. There are a lot of them online. Since I got back from New York, *it* is taking more risks than ever, because I've seen them with my own eyes. I've talked, laughed, danced with them. Some of them even seemed happy. I know I've promised myself not to do it anymore—I really am going to stop—but it's not easy. One of the quotes I dug up during my online Islam expedition is so true. It's from the Islamic scholar Ibn al-Qayyim: "Sight arouses a thought; the thought arouses a desire; the desire arouses a will. And the will grows stronger and stronger until it becomes a deed."

I haven't been here for a couple of weeks, in this second home of mine. It's perfect here: the computers are relatively closed off from each other, it's cheap, it's close to home, and the owner is cool. This internet café, on Kinkerstraat, feels safe. I didn't come here for a while, because of the spitting incident.

It was a typical weekday night. I had a good spot, in the corner—little room for prying eyes there. A little old Turkish man was sitting next to me—digitally challenged, based on the irregular tapping I heard from his keyboard—trying some things out. No one else was around, so my natural sense of watching my back against voyeurs flagged. I was completely in my own world when the man stood up, thunderstruck. One word after the other sputtered out of his mouth in Turkish. He was cursing. I quickly closed the window of the chat room, and my head exploded. Had he secretly been watching? I never go to porn sites, but maybe he saw nudes—they have a way of popping up uninvited. He stood in front of me but refused to look me in the eye—he must have been so disgusted with me. Seconds before it happened, I knew what was coming—this wasn't the first time. I didn't even try to avoid it. From the depths of his throat, he drew spit and hawked it right in my face.

The owner of the internet café heard some noise, but he didn't see that the man had spat on me. He and a few other customers didn't see what was going on. The man paid his bill and slammed the door behind him. While I wiped the spit off my face and logged out, I saw that amid all the commotion, his computer was still logged on. On the screen, I didn't see any Turkish news or family photo collection from Turkey, as I had expected. He had been looking at photos of naked girls—young girls. I paid my bill, put my headphones in, and walked home in the company of a prerolled joint and a can of Smirnoff Ice. On the way home, I promised myself never to do this again.

The guy I'm chatting with right now is someone like me. He sounds cool, and says he's discreet and serious. And he has his own house, whereas most live with their families. He wants to see a photo, but there's no way that's happening. The last time I sent one to a Moroccan guy, he asked: "How are your brothers doing?" right before logging off. I thought my life was over. But I'm no better myself. A while back, I planned to meet up with someone at the tram stop right by the internet café. When I saw from a distance that it was someone I knew, I turned and walked away. I always have to watch out that no one's looking over my shoulder at the screen and make sure that the person I'm chatting with isn't someone I know.

If someone calls me while I'm here, I quickly go outside, so that they can't hear the tapping of the keyboards, and lie about where I am. Everyone complains that they hardly see me anymore.

Should I meet up with this guy from the chat or not? Yes, no, yes.... I don't know. The last time I met up with a Moroccan guy, something happened that I don't ever want to happen again. He came from Eindhoven, in the south of the country, all the way to Amsterdam in his van. I got in and saw two car seats and some toys on the backseat. I still can't erase that image from my head. I checked his hand and saw a wedding ring. He is a father and husband. What the hell am I doing?

"Sorry man, I think I'm gonna go...."

He tried to stop me, but I hopped out quickly and walked home fast—in almost two hours, because we arranged to meet in a remote parking lot and I didn't have money for the night bus. He kept driving behind me until I got rid of him. I didn't go to the internet café for a week after that. I don't know what I expect to find by meeting people this way. None of them are going to help me cure *it* or give me some magical formula to deal with it. The only thing they want is sex. I'm not being honest with them, and sooner or later it'll catch up with me.

The guy I'm talking to now is on Bestevaertstraat in the de Baarsjes neighborhood, not far from Kinkerstraat. He's interested. I like cybersex, but once I'm with them in person, I freeze. This led me to serious trouble, so I need to be more careful. I chug my fourth vodka, light a joint, and turn on my iPod. When I'm almost at the door, the cacophony in my head begins.

You might know him.

What if this is a trap?

Maybe he's crazy.

Why don't you stop this?

You swore it, remember?

Maybe he's ugly.

Shame on you.

I can't even count on two hands how often I've done a U-turn, but the weed and the vodka are doing their thing. I ring the bell and walk two floors up. The door is partly open.

"Lock the door behind you."

In the dimly lit living room, there's not one guy, but two. There's a mirror on the table in front of them with a folded white paper, a credit card, and a couple lines of coke. They're good-looking. The other guy is Turkish. The Moroccan is snorting and asks if I want some too. I politely decline: I've never done it, and I'm starting to feel jittery, despite the THC and my blood alcohol level. He looks offended and does another line.

"Let's go to the bedroom. Two handsome boys just for you."

The Turkish dude does a line of coke too, and they walk ahead of me into the bedroom. They undress down to their boxers and hop on the bed. They leave room free between their muscular bodies, a clear sign for where I should go. I don't move. Whatever sexual tension there was online is now gone. I want to leave, but how? Why do I want to go? Isn't this what I'm looking for?

"Sorry, I'm leaving."

The Moroccan jumps up and grabs me by my neck. "Are you kidding?"

"I'm too nervous. Sorry...."

I try to pull my hand free, but it doesn't work—he's much stronger than I am. His eyes glisten, but no one's home. From the bed, the Turk looks a bit embarrassed and tries to calm him down. It's not working. The Moroccan drags me out of the bedroom, through the kitchen, and out to the balcony.

He pushes me with my torso over the railing of the balcony. My feet unwillingly leave the ground, and I'm looking straight down at the pavement. I've heard that people with cocaine in their bodies get overconfident. Maybe he'll really do it—maybe I'll end up as a stain on the pavement. I look down and feel nothing, and I don't make any effort to calm him down or scream for help. This is the only way to stop *it*—I've tried so many other ways.

Then I hear the Turk behind me. He wraps his arms around his friend's chest and pulls him back to the living room. Then he grabs my shoes and points me to the door. In the hallway, I hear the Moroccan scream: "I know who you are! If I hear anything about this, I know who to look for, you prick!"

They say that if you stop sinning, express regret, and are determined to keep it from happening again, Allah forgives you. I try again to stop going to the internet café, but I only last for a few days. The period between a bad encounter and a new attempt gets shorter and shorter.

"I swear it, if you send your photo, I'll reply."

"You first."

"No, *you* first."

"Well, then never mind."

"Later."

Chats often end up like this, but what's strange is that the moment we both put our foot down, we begin another conversation. Maybe we feel safe enough to share more of our personal life when we know that we're not going to see each other. A lot of times, these guys are involved in prostitution or selling drugs under the name "chems." One of them tells me how he arranged to meet someone in a park at night and was surrounded by three other guys who robbed and beat him unconscious. Another tells about a failed suicide attempt after he learned that he was infected with HIV. His mother found him just in time. As heavy as the conversations are, I find them comforting too.

Sometimes it's like the Big Bang of the internet really created humanity. There's a lot more than Adam and Eve. Even though they were invisible my whole life, people like me exist, trapped in the virtual shadows. When I chat with them, it makes me think of the Morlocks from X-Men, named after the fictional underground characters from

H. G. Wells's science fiction novel *The Time Machine*. The Morlocks are a community of deformed mutants, different from the athletically built X-Men, with their special powers, so they choose an existence in the tunnels under New York. The X-Men don't care much about their fate. The Morlocks are essentially a minority within a minority, accepted neither by their own community nor by the majority, leading them to experience self-hate and resentment. They fall into one tragedy after the next.

Clyde, a Surinamese-Indian classmate from the Reformed Lyceum West and one of my best friends, wants to put an end to his underground existence. Sitting outside of his father's house, he tells me about his feelings toward boys. It's as if the words that come out of his mouth have wrinkles and gray hairs, and are being held up by a wooden cane. They've journeyed a lifetime before arriving, exhausted, at this bench. I say that it's completely fine, but I accidentally add something stupid.

"You don't have to share it with everyone, Clyde, you can also keep it to yourself."

He looks at me, and I quickly ask if he's told his parents and brothers. I've been asked about his sexual orientation before, and I always steered away from answering. They suspect it of me as well. Faera, an old Indonesian classmate and also one of my best friends, said that a couple of guys in our circle of friends had asked him about it once too. He answered that he wasn't sure about Clyde, but that in my case, he'd "bet his life on it." When I tell my mother or brothers about Clyde's coming out, they seem cool with it. They like Clyde a lot, and this doesn't change anything. Faera's words put me at ease— they mean that I've kept *it* well hidden. My mother and brothers, on the other hand, worry me. Are they now saying that they don't have any problem with *it*?

I'm studying Media and Culture at the University of Amsterdam. I'm doing well—I've passed the introductory level and am learning how movies are made through the Film and Visual Culture track. I still want to be a filmmaker. I don't go to the internet café during the day. Only when it's dark out do I spend hours in chats and nonstop discussions about *allochtonen*, or "foreigners"—especially Muslims. When it's light out, I collide with reality; in the dark, I can act as if *they* don't exist. The dates continue, inside and outside of Amsterdam, but no longer with Moroccan-Dutch guys. Every time, I hope to find one who has found a better way to deal with this than I have. Every time, *it* ends up feeling more hopeless. The last time, it led to a stalker, who started to send scary texts when I stopped answering his calls and followed me all the way to my street once when I ran into him by chance.

Before I arrive at an address, I chug my last vodka and take a quick hit from a joint. I also always have poppers with me, because I need the high. Sometimes it's just talking, and sometimes it's more. It doesn't make any difference if the sex is really good or the guy is very attractive. Either way, I feel dirty afterward.

"What's your real name? I'm …"

I never give my name, and I make as little eye contact as possible.

"Can we turn the lights out? Or dim them more?"

If not, I come up with an excuse to cut it short and leave. Once I'm back in my own bed, I recite every *surah* from the Koran I know. I look up to the heavens from an increasingly steep mountain of shame.

"*Ya Rabbi*, this really was the last time."

When night falls the following day, I'm back in the internet café. I want more. Until *it's* gone.

9

Are they cussing out Muslims, or am I paranoid? It's difficult to take everything in amid this racket of whistling, drumming, and jeering. I'm standing with Emre in the middle of a crowd on Dam Square, because Theo van Gogh was killed today in broad daylight by a guy from my neighborhood, Mohammed Bouyeri. He shot van Gogh, slit his throat, and stuck a death threat in his chest, directed at Ayaan Hirsi Ali—an ex-Muslim, Somali-Dutch politician—because the two of them had supposedly offended Allah and the Prophet in their film *Submission*. How he would know that they were offended is beyond me. I'm second-guessing myself about coming—maybe they don't want to see people like me here at all. But this is all so terrible that I have to show my face. I tread extra carefully in the crowd to find a spot. My timidity is annoying me. I see a handful of other Moroccan-Dutch people, and they look as insecure as I do. While I'm listening to the mayor and the Minister of Integration and Immigration, Rita Verdonk, I feel eyes burning into my back and pointed fingers boring into me. Or is that my conscience nagging me? The first thing I thought about when I heard the news was not the victim, but the perpetrator. This flaw has been in my system since 9/11. I don't know this guy at all, but I still somehow feel guilty.

Around our house, it's journalists and cameras everywhere. The last time they came here to snoop around was in 1998, when riots broke out. A garbage can had been set on fire on August Allebé Square, and a kid from the neighborhood who was standing next to it was brutally arrested. Everyone went out on the street to protest against the police. I threw a stone at them too, for all of the times that they'd chased us away when we were just hanging out, when we weren't doing anything wrong. It's kind of weird when I think about it. An officer forcefully grabs a kid who didn't do anything wrong, and I throw a stone at officers who also haven't done anything wrong. Now they're talking about "Mohammed B.'s neighborhood." In an online discussion, I make a comparison to the murder of Pim Fortuyn, an anti-Islam politician killed in 2002 by a white animal rights activist.

"No one was talking about his killer Volkert van der Graaf's neighborhood. So why now with Mohammed Bouyeri?"

The online tug-of-war plays out like I'm used to, but one particular reaction, for which I have no good answer, follows me home from the internet café.

"You're upset about the way they're speaking about Muslims, but where is your rage about what Mohammed B. did?"

Everyone thought that Mohammed Bouyeri was a quiet kid, and look what he did. People are afraid—they no longer know who's a quiet kid and who isn't. Can you blame them? I have to do more than just discuss things online. What good is it doing, spending time reminding people that not all soccer fans are hooligans or parsing out verses from the Koran? Emre recently asked me to go with him again to the Dutch Turkish Workers Association (HTIB), where his uncle is the chairman. The association is housed in a beautiful building in the city center, a few minutes from the world-famous Rijksmuseum, Van Gogh Museum, and Stedelijk Museum. It's not the first place you'd expect to find one of the first migrants' organizations in the Netherlands. The HTIB was founded to protect the rights of Turkish "guest workers." That was back in 1974; now it's 2004. Most of the children of the guest workers are now adults. We have a different outlook on life than our parents. They wanted to earn money and go home, but "going home" for me means taking the train to my hometown in the Netherlands. I don't call myself Moroccan.

I'm "Moroccan-Dutch." When I look at my circle of friends, it's more United Nations than Little Morocco, and it's the same for Emre—he doesn't live in Little Turkey.

My mom keeps asking the same thing every day. "What are they saying about us?"

The neighbor above has become a walking warning sign. Every time I run into him, he grabs me tight, as if we could be deported at any moment.

"Study, work, and go home. Just keep to yourself. They're angry with us."

He means well, but I'm getting more and more annoyed at these kinds of comments ... at the whispering. Whether it's my mother at home or acquaintances from the neighborhood, everyone starts whispering as soon as the conversation turns to the misery that Mohammed Bouyeri has caused. Do they really think that we're being listened to and that secret agents will grab us by the collar at any moment if we speak openly?

At the HTIB, it's anything but whispering. I'm spending more and more time there, and that's mostly because of "M&M." M&M are Mohammed Rabbae, a former Green-Left MP and now chairman of a sort of Moroccan HTIB, and Mustafa Ayranci, the chairman of the HTIB. I often observe them from a distance. Mustafa keeps thinking that my name is Toffel, no matter how many times I say that it's Tofik.

"Toffel, we've been fighting for equal rights for years. Now it's your turn."

Every time one of them says something to me, I think of my father. They probably came to the Netherlands around the same time that he did. Their accent, clothes, and body language all resemble his. Mustafa always gives me a big hug when I come in. At first, I pulled back, but now I don't want to. I act as if he really is my father. When M&M sit still, they look like souvenirs from a lost time of rolled-up sleeves and marches to fight the power, but when they get the microphone at a meeting or gathering, they transform. You can see them get fired up until their eyes start glistening. The words forge a path through a thick accent that still clings to the motherland after all these years. They demand equality every chance they get because they are "Dutch citizens." Whenever they finish speaking, the corners of their mouths curl and their eyes dance for a fleeting moment.

Then their fingers slacken, after having been clenched into fists, and the lines in their skin become visible again. I see that the years have left their mark on them.

"We have to become more active, Emre. They're getting tired."

"That's what I've been saying—I'm ready. But you have to want it too."

"I want it."

I start to ask for the microphone during public debates. We debate with people like Mayor Job Cohen; Secretary of Education, Culture, and Science Mark Rutte—the future prime minister; and my favorite—Rita Verdonk. In the beginning, I stuttered a bit, but I'm starting to feel more and more at ease. I've had three successful confrontations with her—to loud applause—about things that she's said in the media, such as: "The Muslim community can't deal with criticism the way others can."

After our third confrontation, she invites me to her ministry. This way, Verdonk says, I'll have more time and space to explain to her what's bothering me about her policies. That's a smart move on her part: now it will be more difficult for me to criticize her in public the next time.

At the end of a debate, people come up to me and say, "You really need to go into politics."

When I see a debate on TV, I fantasize that I'm in the middle of Parliament at the interruption microphone and verbally thrash Verdonk, Ayaan Hirsi Ali, and the anti-Islam politician Geert Wilders, especially when I see how proud M&M look when Emre or I or one of our friends picks up the mic. If we went into politics, they would be so proud of us. Then they could be at peace, knowing that they could pass the baton. Emre wants to try it. The municipal elections are soon, and he wants to run for the Amsterdam city council for the Labor Party (PvdA). In his attic room, we write the texts for his candidate's statement, presentations, and debates, and we work on what the connecting thread of his story should be.

"Why the PvdA and not one of the other left or progressive parties?"

It takes a while, but then we find a good distinction between the PvdA, on the one hand, and the Green-Left, Socialist, and liberal-democratic D66 parties, on the other: "Dreaming is good; doing is better."

With his Amsterdam accent and alpha-male attitude, Emre fascinates the PvdA members in the meeting rooms. The time has come for the party members to decide which candidates will appear in which order on the election list—almost like an *American Idol* for politicians. At a podium on the Pepsi Stage in Amsterdam-Southeast, a few people are allowed to give an endorsement for Emre. He asks me to be one of them. In front of me, I see councilmen Ahmed Aboutaleb and Lodewijk Asscher, two people I look up to. I've never been so nervous. I'm not exactly sure what I'm saying, but it comes from the heart, and it gets thunderous applause. Everyone who endorses Emre is doing a great job. He gets the eighth spot on the list. March 7, 2006, the day of the elections, the PvdA has significant gains across the Netherlands; in Amsterdam, they're the largest party, with twenty seats. Emre's been elected.

In the meantime, the public debate is becoming obsessed with questions like who Dutch Muslims are having sex with, how many kids they have, what language they speak at home, which TV programs they watch, who they include in their circles of friends and acquaintances, how they greet each other, whether they cheer for the Netherlands or their country of origin during a soccer match, and whether or not everything is "Enlightened" enough. We're being talked about as if we are a single person whose first and last name is simply "Islam."

The only person who really speaks to me in the debates, every time I hear her, is the woman with the black curls from Green-Left, Femke Halsema. Green-Left is also Mohammed Rabbae's party. My brothers are starting to notice how much I've changed at home.

"Are you watching politics again?"

"*Shh!*"

In addition to what "they" are saying about "us," my mother wants to know about Femke Halsema's origins.

"Fimke Maghrebia?"

"For the thousandth time, Mom, she isn't Moroccan."

"Why does she support us then?"

The more I read in the internet café about the history and values of all of the political parties, the more Green-Left fits like a glove. If I had to choose a party, it would definitely be Green-Left. I can barely believe how I went from being someone who was completely disinterested in politics to a political junkie. I chat online less and less. Not just because of the trouble I keep getting in, but because of something else.

Since I've started thinking and debating about the ethnic and religious parts of my identity, it feels like I'm doing something good with my life—something that's vitally important in this climate. I'm good at this.

"You can't forget where you come from, Toffel."

"I won't forget, Mustafa *amca*."

"Then you need to go into politics too and fight for our rights."

If I seriously want to do this, *it* has to go away. The people who are proud of me now, like M&M or those who clap for me when I speak—what would they do if they knew?

You really think they'd still like you then?

They would take away my roots and my religion and only see *it*.

Where does that leave me? *It* has been nothing more than wandering, tipsy, high and numb, from empty encounter to empty encounter, looking for Allah knows what. *It* is bruises and bloody lips. *It* is the eternal confessional box. *It* has only caused confusion and sadness. I'd rather hold on to the sound of a teapot held high in the air, from which a stream of tea lands in the middle of colorful glasses; I prefer to hold on to the serene peace that comes over me when my mother puts on a DVD of Koran recitations on Fridays. *It* can't compete with the moment when I enter the house that my father was born in—ochre-yellow loam with a straw roof, in the Sahara—and his sisters pour out a bottle of perfume on my brothers and me as a sign of happiness and hospitality. *It* can't coexist. I have to choose.

This time for real.

Especially now that the ruling cabinet has stumbled, out of nowhere, over Ayaan Hirsi Ali's passport. She said on TV that she lied on her asylum application about her name and age. Rita Verdonk immediately announced that Hirsi Ali had received Dutch citizenship illegally, after which Hirsi Ali gave up her MP position. Parliament held an emergency debate the same day and forced the minister to "reconsider" her conclusion. Ten days later, "Iron Rita" turned out to be made of elastic. The passport remained intact, but she blamed it all on Hirsi Ali. Hirsi Ali herself admitted as much in an official statement, but it seems to have been signed under pressure. A new debate followed. Femke was killing it: she pushed and pulled endlessly on the cabinet and finally got a motion of no confidence. D66 supported the motion and pulled its political support so there was no longer a majority for this government. The cabinet crashed. At the end of November, right after my birthday, there will be new national elections.

From this moment on, the websites of the political parties have open calls: candidates can now apply for Parliament. I click on the link constantly, read all of the requirements, and close the page.

Just imagine if . . .

I could prove to the kids in the neighborhood, and similar neighborhoods across the Netherlands—kids who think that everyone in politics doesn't care about them or looks down on them—that they're wrong. I could honor the generation of M&M. I could show white Dutch people that the multicultural society is not one big failure. I could take care of my mother and my brothers. I could finally be rid of *it*, because *it* wouldn't dare exist.

I register myself as a party member without telling any of my family or friends. M&M help me get the required signatures from fifteen Green-Left members. On the last day of the candidate application process, I go to the internet café early. I never go this early—the owner looks surprised.

Why do I want this? What do I have to offer? Think hard, Tofik … think hard.

I want Dutch people of color, especially Dutch Muslims, to be seen as individuals. And I want the multicultural generation to which I belong to start thinking, talking, and deciding about all of the things that matter to our collective future, not just integration. I write these ideas in a candidate statement, which I send to the email address on the website, along with my CV, right before the deadline. I check countless times to make sure that I typed the email address correctly and then hit "send." The thought occurs to me that somewhere in the Netherlands, the election commission is looking at my statement and CV and bursting with laughter, making fun of me. About two weeks later, my phone rings while I'm riding in the car with Emre. It's one Hester van der Putte. I know the name from somewhere.

Green-Left!

Short and sweet, she invites me for an interview with the election commission.

10

The train is almost empty, so why would I ride first class? Not having the stress of riding the tram to the University of Amsterdam without paying is great, but this new luxury feels strange. I always catch someone riding in the same train compartment looking at me as if trying to solve a math puzzle. I never know if they recognize me, or if they're wondering what the hell I'm doing in first class. At the same time, I don't want anyone to think that I feel like I'm *all that*, now that I'm an MP.

I step inside a second-class compartment. My ribs still hurt, but no one has the slightest suspicion about what happened in New York. The two guys who have been watching me from a distance at the station enter through the same entrance—do they recognize me? I doubt it. I've only been on TV a couple of times. One of them is about my age, wearing a white djellaba and a thick, full beard. The other is about eighteen, wearing a dark djellaba with jogging pants and sneakers underneath. His beard is having a hard time showing … only a few tufts have popped up here and there.

They follow me to my seat.

"*As-salamu alaykum.* You're Tawfiq Dibi, right?"

"*Alaykum salam.* That's quite perceptive of you."

"We've seen you on TV."

The only thing I can think of that they might know me from is the undercover story. My younger brother Aziz and I went to the party area of Amsterdam armed with hidden cameras and microphones for *Editie NL,* a news program on one of the major Dutch networks. We were turned away from the first four bars and clubs we tried to go to. We didn't have a member card, one of the bouncers said; the others said it was full or didn't even bother to give an explanation. One of them called my brother "ape head" because he asked why we were turned away. Two reporters from *Editie NL,* wearing almost the same clothes as we were, got into all four bars and clubs right after us without any problem. It's the first time that I've made the news as an MP, and there were real political consequences. It even got covered in a newspaper in Morocco. I've been looking forward to this for over a decade. Finally, we had it all on camera, with witnesses.

"Brother, we'd like to talk to you. Can we sit next to you?"

I nod and watch two pious young men turn into starstruck school-girls for a moment as they sit down.

"We're happy that a brother is in Parliament. There's just one thing … something we've seen…."

"Okay … what is it?"

So, it's not about the undercover story? Without exception, I've only had positive reactions from kids like them.

"Look, we're not allowed to go to places like that."

"What kind of places?"

"Didn't you do a story on clubs with a hidden camera?"

"Oh, you mean …"

"We need to motivate our youth to walk down the right path—not lead them toward *el haram.* I hope you understand us."

He's the only one talking, but he's using the we form.

"I had to do something, because when kids like us or from another ethnic background want to go out—when they choose to go out—they need to be treated the same as everyone else."

"I understand what you're saying, but I hope that you understand us too. You have an important position, and you need to be a good role model."

The rest of the train ride, they sit silently across from me, until they say goodbye politely and exit. I expected criticism from people who would point to the problems that some Moroccan-Dutch club-goers cause when they go out. I definitely never saw this coming ... but what's new?

Less than six months ago, I gave my inaugural speech in a debate with none other than Minister Verdonk. She remembered me. In the halls where I ran into her at the HTIB meetings, she could basically ignore me, but here, she had to answer my questions. Afterward, other MPs and staff from our faction waited for me with flowers, because this was the first time that I had spoken in the great hall of the Dutch Parliament. In these moments, it feels like I have a new family. "Farewell, Verdonk Cabinet" was the headline in *Metro* magazine, which featured an interview with me about the new government, in which she no longer had a position. Femke and Mariko, a very smart Japanese-Dutch diplomat, also new in Green-Left, were very happy with it. They say I have a good political antenna.

I have my own office. It's the smallest of the seven MPs, but still, it's an office of my own. I have policy staff members who help me prepare for all of the debates. I have a personal assistant who manages my calendar. Aides walk around in formal wear asking me what I want to drink. The first time that an aide held open the doors to the great hall, with the blue seats, I said it really wasn't necessary and tried to open the door myself. He blocked my way and made it clear that this was his job.

Online, I see some people comment that the only reason I'm an MP is because of my ethnic background. They say I didn't deserve the seventh place on the list of candidates. The members of Green-Left only gave me the spot at their convention because they're "minority-huggers," suggesting it was affirmative action. My background probably played a part, but it's not why I was chosen. I've been involved in politics since 9/11: thinking about social questions, writing and debating about them, coming up with ideas, and putting them into action through volunteering. I know I can do this—that's how

I convinced them. But people online are commenting on way more than that. They are also speculating about *it* on very popular sites like GeenStijl and Maroc.nl. I wonder if my brothers and friends read all of this too. I hope not.

What will I say if a journalist asks about *it?*

I don't know, but I need to think of something. Before you know it, a journalist will ask, or there will be someone from *De Telegraaf* with a fake story. I don't want to think about it. I need to do my job and master the craft of politics, like Femke says.

That's going smoothly. I'm a member of the Dijsselbloem Commission. We're launching a parliamentary inquiry into three education reforms that were passed in the 1990s: secondary education, the pre-university system, and the vocational education system. I myself did the reformed secondary track. We do background studies, examine old parliamentary debates, talk to people who were involved, and organize meetings across the country. Soon we're going to question former ministers, and I'll be one of the MPs interrogating them as well. During the conversations with stakeholders, several people point out how little attention was paid in the nineties to the influx of minority students and the growth of special education students. It immediately makes me think back to the Mercator School.

There are representatives from most of the parties in the commission. Martin Bosma is the brains of the Party for Freedom (PVV), Geert Wilders's party, according to many journalists. He is one of the funniest people I've ever met. Even the otherwise straight-faced Cynthia Ortega-Martijn of the socially conservative Christian Union (CU) cracks up when he makes a joke. How can someone so funny hate Muslims so much?

"Why don't you ever go on TV instead of always having Geert do interviews?" I ask. "I think you'd do really well." "I have a wife and two young kids. I don't want to take any risks."

I don't know what to say to that. Somewhere inside, a feeling of guilt about the things that other Muslims do—a feeling that I've tried to fight off for years—resurfaces for a moment. The fear of Muslims in the Netherlands just won't let up; it's getting worse by the day. Geert Wilders is working on a film that warns about the dangers of Islam. Everyone is talking about it because they're saying he's going to tear up a Koran in it.

"Can't you debate him, Tofik, and explain that he shouldn't talk about Islam like that—that the terrorists aren't real Muslims?"

I've gotten this type of question so many times at Lost, a hookah lounge where, late at night, I blow off steam ... and inhale. They're worried about what will happen in the Netherlands when Wilders's film comes out.

"I'll try my best."

I follow the news more closely than ever before. MPs compete to be the first to raise a particular issue. Whoever is first can use their political weapons first against the ruling coalition. I can present written questions to a minister, who then has at most six weeks to respond. I can summon a minister to Parliament during the Tuesday oral consultation hour or for an emergency debate. And with a majority, I can pass a motion that forces a minister to do or not to do something. But issues that come up in the news aren't just weapons against power; they're also ammunition for media attention. That's important, because political ideals also belong outside Parliament. The fastest MP is always the one that gets a phone call from a journalist and sees their name and quote in a news report. The issues that I speak on in Parliament are integration, education, culture and science, and youth and family. On Monday, together with my staff, I prepare for debates and we think of ideas for our own initiatives, all of which I read up on. Tuesday, Wednesday, and Thursday are filled with meetings and debates in various parliamentary rooms named after dead people, and the weekend is the time for work trips across the country.

In the books that I'd taken to Cuba for preparation, including Montesquieu and the nineteenth-century liberal Dutch statesman Johan Rudolf Thorbecke, I've read a lot about how important it is to have checks on governmental power. I try to keep that in mind during every debate, but it seems to be more theory than practice. Ministers have multiple officials at their side, and often there are others sitting in another room and still more on the other end of the phone. Every question posed by one of us is cracked open, sorted, and answered by those officials on a sheet. Most of the time the minister reads what's written for him or her on autopilot. I just have a few people working for me. Together we have to analyze tens or even hundreds of thousands of words for Green-Left and come up with our political alternative. I'm very lucky with my staff. Noortje and Christel are hilarious, smart, and not scared of me, like many staff are of their MPs. I know that I'm getting better because of them. We usually have four minutes and two interruptions to butt heads with ministers. In the hallways, I sometimes see an MP from a ruling party with an assistant discussing the text of a motion with a minister in order to get his or her political approval. We don't check, we just tickle—and sometimes scratch—political power.

I have to watch out about being too candid with the media. In an interview with *de Volkskrant*, they ask me which part of my portfolio I'm not that excited about. I mention "archaeology." Soon after publication, there's an angry letter from the Dutch Association of Archaeologists. In an interview with *Het Parool* magazine, there's a photo of me in a new DSquared^2 jacket with a fur collar, which I've just bought. I've never bought such an expensive jacket—it cost as much as some people's monthly income. Right after the interview, the advocacy group Fur for Animals sends a letter to Femke telling her I wear fur and that I need to stop, or they'll raise hell. It turns out they're right, when I check the store where I bought it. The fur collar was made from a raccoon. I stop wearing it.

The weekends are no longer normal weekends. I'm constantly scanning the news for reports that I might need to do something about as an MP. It's Saturday. Before I go to chill at Lost, I check the news. I see that three activists from the International Socialists have been arrested in Amsterdam-East because they're walking around with a satirical poster of Geert Wilders. I google the poster and see that Wilders's face has been turned into a pack of Marlboro cigarettes, and the text reads: "Extremist—causes serious damage to you and to society."

Hmm ...

When I was in HTIB, we often helped organize demonstrations, including against the last cabinet's integration policy and against President Bush's foreign policy. I met a number of International Socialists that way. I ask for an email address and suggest that I go with them to Dam Square to protest the arrest with the poster. Soon after, they send an email back.

They want to do it! Femke will kill me, but I'm going to do it. Wilders isn't the only one with freedom of speech.

That day, I get up and take the tram to Dam Square. I haven't said anything to anyone in the faction or at home. There are already a couple of International Socialists holding signboards with the poster pasted on them. I get one too. I'm not quite sure what to do with it. Wave it? Just hold it? Within fifteen minutes, two friendly officers come up to us. They tell us that the poster makes us guilty of libel, and they give us a chance to disperse. We refuse, and a bit later, a van with equally friendly officers comes to bring us to the police station at the Nieuwezijds Voorburgwal, a couple minutes away. We can tell from the way they talk to us that they find this to be ludicrous. When we get to the station, they take us to a cell. I was hoping for more excitement, but it's all pretty boring. In the cell, I feel my phone ring.

Shit—it's Femke. She's probably furious. Should I answer or not?

"Tofik? Is everything okay? Are you in shock?"

How sweet—I thought she'd immediately have my head. It must be in the news, or else she wouldn't know about it.

When I get home, I see that the arrest is getting widely reported. Wilders is against the arrest. I get a letter from the judicial officer saying the charge is dismissed, because "upon closer inspection the poster is primarily a condemnation of Wilders's opinions, and not of him as a person." I feel good: *they* appreciate this, and it shows online too. Who knows ... maybe they'll stop speculating about *it* for a while. I'm happy, but I don't want people to think that I'm only in Parliament representing Muslims or people of color. I also want to do something about the feelings of people like the elderly man on August Allebé Square.

I write an open letter to Geert Wilders for the newspaper. In this letter, I can elaborate on why I felt I had to protest the arrest of those International Socialists.

Dear Geert,

[...]

On September 11, 2001, it was not only airplanes that were hijacked, but also my religious beliefs. In a single day, my personal relationship to Islam was reduced to a viral YouTube video. And my personal life became the target of a-thousand-and-one questions—questions I never got asked before. "What do you really think of Osama Bin Laden?" "Is it true your women are not allowed to shake a man's hand?" "If you had a sister, could she go out, or come home with a white guy?" "Be honest—isn't there something inherently wrong within Islam?"

[...]

I understand that you express the feelings of some Dutch people who no longer recognize their old way of life: Dutch people who see mosques arising and Islamic schools in their neighborhood. They see attacks in New York, London, and Madrid, and they remember the slaughter of Theo van Gogh. They are afraid and shaken. You want to give them a voice. But the Netherlands is made up of more than the people who for you.

[. . .]

I understand that the arrival and permanent settlement of Islam in the Netherlands for many feels like a forced marriage. With marriages, you can—on good or bad terms—divorce. But when there are children involved, the bond is irrevocable, and a good relationship is crucial.

[. . .]

For me, radical Islam is as much of a threat as it is to you. As a free Muslim, I need allies, not enemies.

Geert Wilders doesn't respond, but the open letter gets a lot of coverage, just like the arrest. I see more and more comments about me, online and offline: Moroccan-Dutch people and Dutch Muslims … a lot of them are proud of me. *They* see me as one of them, but every time someone shows me love or a tap on the shoulder in the train, or when I'm shopping or in the hookah lounge, I always think the same thing: "Would you still say that if you knew about *it?*"

The first-class compartment is still an unusual experience. On the way home from a meeting with the Dijsselbloem Commission, three Moroccan-Dutch girls storm by. I'm the only one sitting in the compartment. They see me and stop. They look at each other, mumble something, plop down together on a seat, and sink away into their phones. The conductor comes shortly after.

"Tickets please."

"I told you we had to keep moving, bitch," says one to the other, while they fish their second-class train passes out of their bags.

"Ladies, you're sitting in first class."

"Yeah, but he is too!"

I feel bad, but I show my Parliament-issued first-class pass. The girls stopped and sat next to me because they assumed I didn't have a valid pass either. The conductor is in a good mood. He points sharply toward the second-class car farther down, and they storm away. I want to prove that I haven't forgotten where I've come from—that I'm still the same guy I was before being in Parliament—but that's just not true. With Noortje and Christel, I've written an actual bill to "teach youth to be self-sufficient and well informed in finding their way in a complex, information-based society." Media education would need to be made into a main objective for primary and higher education. The bill's text opens with "Our Beatrix, by God's grace, Queen of the Netherlands, Princess of Orange-Nassau." No more letters from debt collectors "in the name of the Queen," but rather a bill.

I've changed, whether I like it or not.

11

The police want to talk to me. They left a phone number in my weekly mail in Parliament. I have no idea what it's about, but it must be personal. I'm sharing a room with Noortje and Christel at the moment, so I can't call from here. The safest is to go outside. No one can overhear me there. The phone call is short. I need to present myself at the police station on Marnixstraat in Amsterdam.

At the station, I'm met by two men in their forties. One has long hair in a ponytail; he makes me think of the guys I'd see at a Green-Left convention. They work for the financial crimes investigation department.

"You're sending large sums from the Netherlands to Morocco. That rings some warning bells for us."

I'm so relieved! Is that it? I'd imagined the worst kinds of scenarios in my head. In Morocco, I can only withdraw a limited amount per day from the ATM, and since this time I paid for my mother and my two brothers, whom I'd taken on vacation with me, that amount wasn't always enough. I'd also happily helped my grandmother renovate her house. That's why I had used internet banking to transfer money to Clyde's account, which he then deposited in my name via Western Union. I explain all of this to the police in detail, but something's off. They don't seem quite satisfied ... there must be more.

"Our bells don't ring for just anyone when money is transferred."

"Okay ..."

"The reason they rang in your case has to do with your brother Aziz."

" . . . "

"He doesn't run in good circles, so we're keeping an eye on him."

" . . . "

"Do you live together?"

It seems like they're worried about me. They're not just doing their work; they're also trying to warn me in case something happens. If something bad got in the news, it would hurt me, and therefore Green-Left as well. I promise the officers that I will have a tough talk with my brother when I get home.

When I get home, I try for the umpteenth time to convince him to give up the street life and focus on studying. I also tell him, in the hope that this might sway him, that everything he does will affect me too.

"Do you know how often I speak in debates about the criminal behavior of Moroccan-Dutch youth? What do you think they'll say if my brother gets caught up in that mess too? What do you think that would mean for Green-Left?"

The message seems to get through, but the conversation feels somewhat pointless. He has his life and I have mine; it's not like it used to be. I'm not here anymore to watch out for him. When I get home, I'm exhausted and plop into bed, or I stay in my room and prepare for debates. In the mornings, I'm gone before I see anyone.

Meanwhile, I'm being noticed by the media: journalists call me more and more to ask what I think about different issues, and I'm getting requests for big interviews. I spend most of my time in Parliament focusing on youth affairs and education, but the only thing they want to talk about is integration, immigration, and Islam. Some journalists are also digging, trying to find skeletons in my closet. Recently, a journalist from *Elsevier* called for that reason. He apparently discovered that my name is spelled "Tovek" in my passport. He was wondering why, given that it's spelled "Tofik" everywhere else. I laughed—it seemed like he was hoping for a "passport affair" à la

Ayaan Hirsi Ali. I explained to him that my parents had pronounced it "Tawfiq" at my birth, and that it had been turned phonetically into "Tovek." Instantly, I heard his mouth-watering dry up.

Much more subtly, they try to uncover *it*. The question never comes up directly—always through a side route. A journalist from *de Volkskrant* waits until lunch after a big interview and then says, while she holds her fork like a pen: "The guys in the editorial room are wondering ... do you prefer men or women?" In Nieuwspoort, where there's a party right before the parliamentary recess, a journalist from the public broadcaster NOS offers me unlimited vodka-7 Ups, as if it were a truth serum. After a couple of glasses, she asks if I'll kiss one of the guys in the room once I'm tipsy. While I'm walking from Parliament to the station with a journalist from RTL News, she "casually" asks me, "Doing anything fun this weekend? With your girlfriend? Or boyfriend? That's okay too, right?" It happens so frequently that I've come up with a kind of standard answer, a rehearsed line, like politicians often do to avoid tricky questions.

"I know what you're trying to do, but I don't have anything exciting to report."

I often come up in the news in relation to Geert Wilders's party, the Party for Freedom. I don't understand why so many politicians and journalists let that party get away with so much racism—and worse. Martin Bosma, with whom my interactions have become less amicable, comes up to me in the hallway.

"We are the reason for your existence—without us, you don't have a story."

His comment bothers me, because that thought is on my mind as well. If I take a stand against racism and discrimination this week, I feel the pressure to do something with youth affairs or education the next week. Otherwise, both white people and people of color could criticize me for representing only one group. What is my own story, really? What do I have to say about the Netherlands? Why did I go into politics? I write it down as well as I can in a manifesto, which I sign with a group of friends of mine. I call it "So 2001," a reference to how the sociopolitical debate has stalled since September 11, 2001.

[...]

We connect with each other across all barriers. We operate not along ethnic or religious lines, but on the basis of shared interests and ideals. We hang out in the same social scenes, study the same fields, and dream of the same future. Our cradles rocked from the coast of the Black Sea to Amsterdam Old-South, from the heights of the Rif Mountains to Cuijk, in the province of Brabant. To an increasing degree, we are children from mixed families. For us, the presence of cultural and religious difference is as self-evident as breathing. A headscarf on stilettos. Freckles with frizzy hair. Not just double, but triple citizenship.

[...]

We are ready for the next phase in the integration debate, and we ask the political world to follow us.

The future of the Netherlands is tied to the freedom of our generation to be in charge—in charge of our own lives. In the next phase, we are free to throw off the headscarf or wrap it around our heads. We are free to travel to Surinam or Curaçao without being subjected to a full-body search. We are 100% free to criticize the multicultural society without being called a xenophobe or racist. We are 100% free to criticize xenophobia or racism without being labeled "politically correct." We want to be spared from politicians who talk to us every goddamn day about what we're doing wrong by existing and through what hoop we should jump to make them feel better. We refuse to be whitewashed into cultural clones of the prototypical Dutchman, created by the politicians in The Hague: a goody-goody citizen who eats meatballs on Wednesday with the Wilhelmus national anthem playing in the background, complaining about how traditions are being taken away from "us." And we will no longer allow you to relate us to every criminal on the news who happens to share the same ethnicity as us.

It's getting easier for me to voice my political standpoints in the media and in Parliament. There's quite a bit going wrong in youth affairs. I believe that a parliamentary inquiry, like the Dijsselbloem Commission, could help. I want to make it an official request, and Tom suggests that we ask Rita "Corrie" Verdonk, who is an MP now, to be a cosponsor. Noortje, Christel, and I call Verdonk "Corrie" so that she doesn't catch on when we gossip about her. Recently, through a twist of fate, we've moved into an office right next to hers, due to construction in Parliament.

Verdonk agrees, and soon almost all of the opposition is won over. I invest a lot in my youth affairs portfolio—partly because I often think about that day with the children's services office. I'm so thankful to them that they decided to give our mother custody. I can't bear to think how our life would have been if we ended up with that witch of a stepmother or a foster family.

MPs have a weird way of talking. I'm surprised to find myself starting to use nasty expressions that I'd never heard before. "Chairman, it can't be that . . ." or "This is just a cigar from one's own box," or "The minister has butter on his head." On the other hand, some expressions that are completely normal outside of Parliament have a completely different meaning here. I can't just say "you're twisting things and being dishonest" to Education Minister Ronald Plasterk. To be seen as dishonest toward Parliament would be the gravest political sin. A minister would have to step down in that case. I enjoy politics, but I never stay to hang out in The Hague. As soon as I can, I take the train back to Amsterdam. I put my iPod headphones in to listen to music and to avoid the standard conversations, but this trick rarely helps, especially with elderly train-riders.

"You're Tofik Dibi, right?"

"That's right."

"I forget ... are you Moroccan or Turkish?"

"I was born in Vlissingen."

"Oh, really? That's great."

"And are you Moroccan or Turkish?"

"I'm Moroccan-Dutch."

It's quiet for a minute.

"I think it's great that someone like you has made it this far."

"Thank you ... that's kind of you."

"You've taken advantage of all of the chances that this country has given you and made the most of them. That really is impressive."

"Yeah...."

"It's too bad that all of those other kids make such a mess of it—that they throw away their chances here in the Netherlands. Why is that?"

"I don't know. I think it depends on the person."

The conversation with the woman goes on a while longer. I try to stay as polite as possible, but my patience is running out. I've lost count of how many times I've had these kinds of conversations with white Dutch people—even before becoming an MP. I try to imagine what it would be like if I, as a citizen, went up to random white MPs in the train and addressed them the same way.

"You're Mark Rutte, right?"

"That's right."

"I think it's great that someone like you has made it this far."

"Thank you ... that's kind of you."

"You've taken advantage of all of the chances that this country has given you and made the most of them. That really is impressive."

"Yeah...."

"It's too bad that all of those other kids make such a mess of it—that they throw away their chances here in the Netherlands. Why is that?"

Femke can be refreshingly blunt if someone addresses her like that.

It's hilarious. Maybe I need to try it sometime. Recently, someone said to me: "Wow, you speak Dutch really well." "You too," I replied.

Femke is going to step down. She's been through a lot of turbulence during her twelve years in Parliament and is looking forward to a new phase in her life. It's complicated. On the one hand, I'll miss her political style and work, from which I'm still learning so much. I'll never forget how precisely and fiercely she fought in the debate about the Davids Commission, which investigated the Netherlands's political support for the illegal invasion of Iraq. On the other hand, it's about that time to come out from under her wing and develop my own voice.

She names Jolande Sap as her successor, and we agree unanimously. Jolande is very different from Femke, but I have faith in her too. She is an economist, and since the financial crisis began, integration, immigration, and Islam are no longer the only issues in politics and the media. Ineke—a friend of mine and our longest-sitting MP—and I become the faction leadership, together with Jolande. As an MP, I'm going to be responsible for Asylum and Immigration, Security and Justice, and Agriculture, Nature, and Food Safety. There are days when I have a debate about wild animals in the circus, followed by a debate about sexual abuse in the Catholic Church, and ending with a debate about children asylum-seekers who are being threatened with deportation. My life consists of work, work, and more work. I hardly see my family or friends.

On the tram, after a discussion panel in Amsterdam, I go past the internet café. It's been years … I'm curious what it's like now. I look inside and see that it's almost empty. I get off at the next stop. I just want to take a look—no more.

"Hey man! Long time no see. How's it going?"

"Yeah man, things are good. How are you?

"I'm good too. I see you on TV sometimes or in the newspaper. You're doing a good job."

"Thanks, man."

I go sit at my favorite spot, with my back covered. From here, I can see everyone who comes inside. The online chats are still as direct as I remember. The only things that are different are the djinns. They've multiplied—there are a lot more of them than before. They still have no faces or names. I'm busy chatting with a couple of them. I didn't realize how much I've missed this contact—the hours fly by. One keeps asking for my photo and swears that he'll send his back, and that he's discreet. He's already sent one of his body. I close my eyes and press "send."

"Seriously?"

"What?"

"Do you think I'm crazy?"

"Why would I?"

"Aren't you that politician from Green-Left?"

Shit.

Inside and outside Parliament, I defend the rights of lesbian, gay, bisexual, and transgender people with a passion. I do so above all because I truly believe it's the right thing to do. But it's more than a political ideal: defending a freedom that I don't allow myself is a way to clear my conscience, for not having the strength to be a mirror for people like myself. And it's the ultimate disguise. I hope everyone thinks: "How could someone who's so progressive want to keep something like that secret? He must not be *it*."

12

"Tofik Dibi Faggot" in bright rainbow colors moves slowly from left to right on a gigantic plasma display in So, one of the most popular clubs in Marrakesh. It's Friday, and it's packed. I see familiar faces from the Netherlands in line, and inside, I see a guy who cuts my hair sometimes. The screen is above the stage, and club-goers can write short messages there. There are lots of "hi's" and "I love you's," but now it says "Tofik Dibi Faggot." I close my eyes and open them again. It's really there. It's as if I'm standing naked on the playground of my high school during the break.

The disorientation lasts a while before I understand it. It's the guy who was lurking around me earlier. He must have tipped the guy working the screen, because this text stays longer than the other messages. When I came in and got a table, I saw him staring. He's a hefty guy with a black T-shirt, a black cap, and a drink in his hand. When I was just at the bar ordering our mojitos, he came up behind me and put his hand on my shoulder.

"Why do you speak badly about Islam?" he asked, as the stench of his Bacardi and Coke desecrated my nose. I didn't know what he was talking about, but I pushed his hand away.

"Don't touch me, moron!"

He began shouting things, and people came between us and broke it up. He disappeared into the crowd and I went back to our table. My cousin Fouad and Rachad, the daughter of a childhood friend of my mother, see that I'm shaken and ask what's going on. Embarrassed, I tell them what's on the screen. They immediately go up to the person taking requests and tell him what's up. He erases the text. They ask me if I know who did it. The guy is still staring, but now looks amused. I point him out. They run toward him like crazy people, and a security guard follows them. I pull them back and say that I don't care. They don't listen—they want him kicked out of the club, or they'll kill him. He makes excuses, drunkenly trying to explain why he did it, but the guard points him to the door. I explain to Fouad and Rachad that I'm used to this kind of stuff, and I force out a fake smile that would put all other fake smiles in the world to shame.

Tofik, did you really think they'd accept you if you just fought hard enough against discrimination and racism?

I don't know if I seriously expected that, but I secretly hoped so, ever since my first day in Parliament, when a colleague from the Labor Party asked me in the elevator if I was an intern. I hoped that *it* wouldn't matter if I just showed them how much I cared for *them*. Maybe they would even accept *it*. I know a lot of people value what I do—I hear it almost daily. But somehow it's always the others, like this moron, whose validation I crave. I want to show *them* how much I love Allah, that I'm not going to betray my roots, that I'm a real man. I want to prove myself to *them*, but it doesn't matter: *it* will erase everything I do and what I most believe in.

The following night, when I'm wandering through Guéliz on the way to an internet café on a side street off of Djemaa el Fna to check my parliamentary email, a guy starts talking to me. He's my age, and he is looking mighty fine. It seems like he's trying to flirt with me, based on his manner of talking. I smile and keep walking, but he follows.

"*A zin*," he says—which means "beauty"—"why don't you want to talk to me?"

Across from the horse stables at the edge of Djemaa el Fna, I go to the side of a busy park to fiddle with my phone. He'll leave eventually if I ignore him, I think. It's futile. He won't give up—he comes to sit right next to me.

"Difficult, this, right? For us it's much harder."

He immediately saw that I wasn't from Morocco, as they always do. He keeps talking and explains that he came to Marrakesh to earn enough money to travel to another country. It's hard to save, because he sends money to his parents every month. Now that he's sitting close, I see that he wouldn't look out of place on the catwalk of a prestigious Italian fashion house.

"Wanna go to a quieter place farther up? You don't have to be afraid—I just want to hold your hand."

I'd sworn off this kind of thing, but the mess in So affected me. Why should I hold myself back? It doesn't matter anyway. And it's been so long. Messing around with women happens every now and then, but it's meaningless. The emotional connection is missing. I stand up and walk with him. We keep talking until we arrive at a bigger park. There, we're far away from the bustle. It's quieter and darker. Without speaking, he points to a large tree farther away, past a little gate. It's difficult to walk through the bushes, stones, and garbage, though it's a lot easier for him. He leans against the tree and winks at me to come next to him. I stand under the tree, but right before the forbidden fruit can be plucked, two silhouettes crawl out from the shadows.

I gasp for air. They must have followed us. "Run," he whispers. Before I can say anything, he disappears. They don't chase after him: they're both coming for me. I try to run away, but I stumble on the rocks and hit the dirt. It's two older men; they're not just some homeless people, based on their clothing. One of them shows a knife, and the other tries to grab my ankle. I kick him hard in the face. He falls back and covers his face with both hands. He swears that he'll butcher me when he catches me. I stumble again after taking a couple of big steps. Now he swears that no one will care if someone like me is found dead. His hot breath burns on my neck. Will it happen this time?

"Here! Here!"

I grab my parliamentary cell phone and throw it as far as I can; I throw the three hundred dirham and some change from my other pocket in the other direction. They both go for the loot. I run as hard as I can in the direction of the lights in the distance until, gasping, I reach Djemaa el Fna. I feel scrapes on my hands, arms, legs, and knees, and a cut above my lip. It's not that bad, but how am I going to explain this to Fouad and the two good friends who are waiting in our apartment, expecting to go out? They must have called me and are probably worried because they didn't hear anything back. I can't believe I've gotten myself into this kind of shit again. I'll just say I got robbed without saying exactly what happened. It works—they buy it. I tell Willemijn, my strict but sweet personal assistant, that I lost my phone in a taxi so that she can block it. When we get to club Paradise, a bouncer gives us a hard time because of the scrapes and cut on my face. That will definitely become a small scar, but if I don't shave for a day, no one will notice. I give the bouncer a hundred dirham and he lets me in.

Back in the Netherlands, I see that that moron from So has mockingly tweeted me about what happened from an anonymous account. He's delighted with himself. In my overfull inbox, I also see an email from the European Foundation for Democracy. They want to know if I'd be willing to be on a discussion panel with Irshad Manji when she comes to the Netherlands in December. She'll be on a tour for her second book: *Allah, Liberty and Love: The Courage to Reconcile Faith and Freedom*. I've heard and read a little about her. I'm not sure if I should do it. She's a lesbian Muslim. *They*'ll certainly think of *it*. But my curiosity trumps my fears, and I'll happen to be in New York in October with a parliamentary delegation at the General Assembly of the United Nations. We plan to connect via Skype and see if we click. As soon as the connection is made, she launches into a conversation. She seems really cool. We arrange for me to visit her at her office at New York University to talk some more about her book and a possible panel.

In New York, after one of the boring political events, I take a taxi to Irshad's office at NYU, where she teaches. I try to be nonchalant, but I can hardly believe my eyes. There she is, in a simple room with a desk and a computer, waiting for me: a Muslim woman who has *it* too. I've never met one who lives openly and freely. She offers home-made chai latte from a thermos, gives me a cookie, and starts talking, full of energy, about the things that she's working on and about her experiences. When she presents her book in Amsterdam, she wants to have a conversation with me about the question of "how reformist Muslims can prevent the Islam debate from being hijacked by extremists, be they Islamophobes or radical Muslims." While she's talking, I ask myself if she suspects *it* of me. I think so.

Should I say it?

I've been looking for so long, since that glimpse in *My Beautiful Laundrette*, and finally someone who's truly free is sitting right in front of me. And she's constantly cracking jokes.

She seems happy. How is that possible?

While she chats, it's like I'm looking into a mirror. Everything that's happened in the past feels less traumatic because of her—this reflection of myself. I'm not the only one, I think, and I look at her. She just seems happy. It's like I'm floating around in her office, feeling so light, imagining a life without all of my inhibitions.

Maybe it's possible?

That's what hope is: to see in another what seems impossible for oneself. I want to stay here. Later, when I crawl back into my own skin and walk outside to catch a cab to meet the other MPs at the hotel, I'll be back to reality.

I'll only see what's impossible; here, I finally see what's possible.

It worked out for her. Why wouldn't it work for me?

The event with Irshad is a couple of months later, on December 8th. I meet her at her hotel in the center of Amsterdam. We're both wearing a white shirt with a red sweater on top. In the cultural forum De Balie, in a room with a modest turnout, we're chatting for a quarter hour when the doors open again. I see about twenty Muslim guys entering—young men in their teens and twenties, in traditional robes, most of them with beards. They come in, observe the room and the stage, and sit down in the back rows. I now count twenty-two. They clearly have some kind of plan, but Irshad and I refuse to stop talking. She invites them to take part in a discussion. They respond in unison with ceaseless, ominous screaming. Noortje is sitting there too. This could easily go the wrong way. We're sitting in a closed space, and if we want to leave, we'll have to go past them first.

"*Takbir!*" one of them screams.

"*Allahu Akbar!*" answer the rest.

They throw eggs, and one of them hits my shoulder.

"*Munafeeq!*"

"*Murtad!*"

"*Kafir!*"

They keep throwing eggs and these kinds of insults, in which they label us fake Muslims or apostates. In some Islamic circles, it's believed that those who leave Islam deserve to be put to death.

Irshad does not back down in any way. She blows kisses to them and waves with her book. When I grab her hand, I feel her shaking. One person in the audience, a young woman with a headscarf, is standing on a chair and shouts at them for misbehaving like this. They shout back at her just as hard and spit in the face of Fouad Sidali, a local Labor Party politician. I can tell that they want to stop us from talking about our religion because for them, we're not Muslims. The other people in the audience stand up as a line of protection between Irshad and me on the stage and the guys in the back of the hall. Two officers come soon after. They ask us to leave the stage in order to deescalate the situation. We refuse. More officers come. Now that it's a bit safer, I can see what's happening more clearly. There are a couple of guys taking the lead in the yelling. They have a black flag featuring the *shahada*, and there's a guy with a camera filming everything. They had planned out their outfits and slogans. These guys aren't following the example of the Prophet—they're living according to the prophetic expression made famous by Andy Warhol: *In the future, everyone will be world-famous for fifteen minutes.*

I often read that in their previous lives, guys who radicalized had ambitions to be drug dealers, rappers, or soccer players. These slogans they keep shouting are echoes of broken dreams. This is their Tony Montana moment: shooting the winning goal in the World Cup, a performance in a sold-out, thundering arena. After this they'll go home, put the video online, and feel like superstars. We stand opposite each other for an hour, until the police buses arrive. The guys are led outside through an emergency exit on the stage. Irshad and I give our report to the police, and afterward, we appear on the TV show *Pauw en Witteman*. In the reactions to what happened, I see people saying that it's urgent to talk about the threat of Islam. They don't seem to realize that at this point, it's the same as saying we really need to discuss the weather.

I can't fall asleep. They're called Sharia4Belgium. It was like a team of supervillains was torn out of a comic and brought to life. You have them in comics too: mutants who attack other mutants because they don't take responsibility for their superior position to other people. The X-Men are constantly in conflict with groups like the Brotherhood of Evil Mutants, who see them as traitors to the race. This was more than that. The guys from Sharia4Belgium have excommunicated us. I'm trying my hardest in politics, for these kinds of guys. I'd walk through fire for their rights. I saw fire in their eyes tonight. Without batting an eye, they'd have thrown Irshad and me into that fire until we burned to ash. Sometimes I just want to give up altogether.

13

"This will be the end of your political career. I think that would be a terrible waste."

I'm sitting in Jolande Sap's living room. She lives here with her husband and children. I can see that I'm hurting her. I feel bad, but I block my emotions. There will be new national elections. I've put myself forward for the political leadership of Green-Left and am therefore challenging Jolande for her position as the sitting leader. I'm not going to let anyone talk me out of this—not Jolande, not Femke, not Tom, not Christel and Noortje. Prominent members of our party whom I have a great deal of respect for drop by or call on the phone.

"What the hell do you know about economics?"

"Finally we have a Moroccan guy who knows what it's like to start from the bottom and climb out of it, and this is what you do!"

"Your time will come—what's your hurry?"

I use their condescending words as fuel to strengthen my position. Every time they question my political prowess—despite the fact that I've been working on every conceivable issue for the past six years—I entrench myself further. Every time I sense that I'm supposed to know my place—the place of the "free-thinking Muslim" and the "successful Moroccan Dutchman"—the earth piles up higher and higher around me. The more people meddle, the less I see; the more they say, the less I hear.

Why am I doing this? Jolande wasn't chosen democratically, but do I really care about that as long as a majority supports her? The way

105

that she put pressure on us to vote for the police training mission in the Afghan province of Kunduz has damaged the trust between us. Ever since, the faction has been plagued by an everyone-for-themselves mentality. But we—or I—could have voted against the mission, despite the pressure. And threatening to pull my support, as I did, has only made the trust issues between Jolande and me worse. I've also been feeling uneasy about what the hunger for being part of the ruling coalition is doing to us. There's something that happens to political parties as they get closer to being in power. They start to resemble each other, talk the same way, and, often, make the same choices. The PVV is the best example of this. The party talks considerably less about Muslims since it became a tolerated consulting partner of the cabinet. If I ask for information about immigration statistics or a debate with Minister of Immigration Gerd Leers, they hide behind all sorts of procedures that they previously treated with disdain. The closer Green-Left gets to power, the more I notice these kinds of traits in us, too. That's why, I think, things are bad in the polls. We're projected to get only half of the seats that we currently have in Parliament. But am I going to be able to turn the tide by challenging the leadership? Is it because all political leaders are white? I dream about more people of color in charge, but is that really why I'm doing this? My biggest statement during my press conference is that Green-Left needs to reinvigorate itself by daring to be different. I truly believe that, but am I the right person to do it?

In any case, I need to get official permission to run first. In the Stopera, the Amsterdam city hall, Jolande and I receive a confidential judgment from the party election commission about our qualifications for the leadership. The judgment is a recommendation to the members of the party. Jolande goes first. I walk into the room, where chairman Tof Thissen and vice chair Patricia Seitzinger are waiting for me. I can see in their eyes what's going to happen. Tof doesn't mince words: I've been found to be unsuitable to run for the leadership. He gives me a letter with the written judgment. I read it, but I can't believe it. *Did you really think that they'd see you as equal, as long as you worked hard enough for them?*

I rip up the letter in front of them and walk out. Then they tell me I have one hour to decide whether or not I want to appeal the decision. *Unsuitable.*

I'm sure all of the racists who've been saying for years that I'm a "cuddle-minority" are popping bottles right now. All of the years that I've worked my ass off for the ideals I believe in, for a party that believed in me: thrown away with a single word. I call Femke and Christel. I pull myself together before they answer so that I don't cry. This is the first time I can remember that I fail at holding back the tears. The years of stress must have taken their toll: the tears make up for lost time. Femke and Christel's advice is to follow all of the procedures. I'm going to appeal.

Tof and I are heard in an emergency session of the appeals and disputes commission. The following day, they come to the conclusion that the judgment of the election committee was made on "a very narrow basis." It doesn't matter. The judgment is already everywhere in the media. Heleen Weening, the party chair, completes the humiliation that night by repeating it a couple of times on the late night talk show *Knevel & Van den Brink.*

They find me to be a "fresh, fun, and appealing person" and "a creative outsider with infectious enthusiasm," but "Tofik doesn't fully understand the in-depth connections among the core values of the party."

That night, I go to Lost for some hookah and a mojito. I've been on TV, the newspapers, and the internet so much that it seems like everyone recognizes me. It's pretty quiet in Lost. While I'm sitting at the bar, a Surinamese-Dutch guy who's often there taps me on my shoulder.

"Let me give you a *brassa*"—Surinamese for a hug.

"Thanks, man."

"You know, I've told you many times—they'll never accept us as one of them."

"…"

It is decided that I can still participate in the leadership referendum despite the verdict "unsuitable." The first debate with Jolande takes place at De Rode Hoed cultural center. There are cameramen, photographers, and journalists everywhere. As I walk in, I run into Jamal, Nourdin, and some of their friends. What a surprise. I've hardly seen them during all of this and kept them out of the loop. Their presence feels like the hot meal and night's rest that I've been missing for weeks. Before I have to go up, I see a group of young Moroccan-Dutch women among the hundreds of Green-Left members. They're not members, so what are they doing here? I walk over and greet them. I don't know them, but I feel closer to them in this moment than I do with my own party members. *I'll always remain a Moroccan.*

Jolande opens the debate with her speech, and then it's my turn. I've been looking forward to this moment. I've saved the file on my computer as my "farewell speech." I haven't told anyone and am still keeping it to myself, but this will be my farewell to these lovely people and this lovely party. I know I'm going to lose, and that will be the end of me in politics.

"It's safe to say that since last week people will no longer be calling us a 'party of minority-huggers.'"

There's laughing and clapping.

Unsuitable.

"Unsuitable. That's what political icon Hans van Mierlo said about our green ideas in 1989. A 'cry in the night,' to be precise."

"You have a kid with a disability? Sorry, this school is unsuitable."

"Self-employed? We don't have any suitable unemployment insurance."

"Guys, you want to come into this club? Maybe that other club is more suitable."

"No residence permit? Unsuitable."

"People who strive for change, who are different, get the door slammed in their faces time after time."

I go on for a while until the hall bursts into thunderous applause. Afterward, the hall doesn't feel hostile anymore. This is just what I needed to refresh myself for the other coming debates with Jolande and the countless media appearances coming up, because I'm a dead man walking. One of the appearances is on *De Halve Maan*, a program that I was supposed to be a guest on last week, but I had to cancel because I was waiting for the judgment of the election commission. They give me more of an opportunity to really speak on what I envision for Green-Left than I get on many other programs that focus on the drama. Suddenly, another guest, the Egyptian-Dutch publicist Monique Samuel, skillfully navigates herself into the conversation.

"I wonder if, in this case . . . Well I think it's safe to say you just got dissed by your party. Don't you agree?"

"By the top of the party. There's a difference between the leadership and the members."

"But the members . . . they'll eventually follow . . . The thing is that they disagree with what your party is doing, but ultimately, they always vote in favor of whatever the leadership says. So, I'm wondering: you knew this would happen. Why did you go on with challenging the leadership knowing they would turn on you?"

"Because I have a problem with party members, or Dutch people for that matter, always following the safe path, always choosing the obvious."

"Okay, but then I have another question for you, because you're saying—okay, following the safe path. I came out of the closet a year ago . . ."

She's not going to say what I think she's going to say on national television?

"And by doing so, I've been an important role model for many people. Now I'm asking you: you're so brave, fighting for the party leadership role even though you really know that you won't win. Then why are you scared to come out of the closet?"

I laugh as lightheartedly as I possibly can. She must have thought about this in advance.

"Why are you scared to come out?"

"I think you set this up."

"No, I didn't set this up, but I've always wondered about it, from the start...."

"You can wonder. Of course. And you can ask the question, but do you know me personally?"

"No, but look, the point is, this question is posed to you all the time. And you deny, deny, deny. But you don't prove the opposite either. And I know a lot of people ... I, I have a double feeling about it ... I'm lesbian ..."

Naeeda Aurangzeb, the host, interrupts, but not in the way I was expecting or hoping.

"Why do you think it's important?"

I have to cut this off myself, because the hosts seem to find this perfectly okay.

"It's irrelevant, in any case. I am who I am. Whatever speculations you have about me don't matter. Why should I have to answer at all if it's so irrelevant?"

"It's actually very relevant, that's why I said it."

"Not if it's not true, right? You want me to be some kind of poster boy for something that you're thinking in your head."

"No, I think that a lot of Dutch people think the same, and that it keeps following you wherever you go."

The other guest on the show, former soccer player Dries Boussata, who had played for AZ Alkmaar with Jamal for a while, tries to help out, with the best of intentions.

"What matters is what kind of politician he is, right?"

Before there's an answer, the other host, Aad van den Heuvel, changes the subject. I know everyone is watching my every move these days, but I hope to hell that my family and friends aren't watching this. I am mortified.

"*It's irrelevant,*" *I said. Wow.*

The fake story in *De Telegraaf* might have finally been scrapped (and the journalist involved was fired for other reasons), but now other journalists smell blood. I get asked the same question, sitting on the couch of Paul de Leeuw's TV show. Before the show, the producer hints at an online comment that says I went to the Arab gay bar Habibi Ana. I've never set foot in there, and tell her so, but the question comes anyway. And again, on the popular *Coen en Sander Show* on the radio.

"Do you like men or women?"

"I like women."

Strictly speaking, I'm not lying—I have been attracted to women often enough—but morally, I am. I can barely keep it up. Luckily, it's time for the results of the referendum. Jolande and I are the first to be informed of the outcome. She wins with 84 percent of the votes, and I get 12 percent. At the press conference, I congratulate her on her "almost Eastern European victory." I tell the journalists dutifully that I want to be her running mate. When I have to go talk to the election commission about my place on the list of candidates for the coming elections, I tell the members that I want to be number 10—an unelectable number. They're visibly relieved—they were worried about having to deal with me.

Soon after the results of the referendum, Monique Samuel is there again with an op-ed in the *NRC Next* newspaper, in which she makes the same kinds of overbearing demands that I've had to deal with for years from emails, from party members, and from people on the street.

"Dibi lost the race for party chairman, but there's another fight waiting for him that he can win. Dibi, be a hero and be a champion for all of those people who want to come out of the closet but are too afraid and need a figurehead like you."

Every person has three lives: a public life, a personal life, and a secret life. Am I only truly free if I make my secret life public? Or is it a sign of freedom if I have the choice to keep it to myself? Do I want to keep living like this? Until something really bad happens? After all, that's what this whole leadership battle stemmed from. I want to lose myself in other things: to be so occupied by my work that I don't hear *them,* and never have to dwell on *it.* The personal is political. I put myself forward as the savior of my party in the hope that I could save it, because I can't save myself.

14

Dear brothers, this letter is meant for all three of you! It's about some-
thing we've never talked about, but something I've thought about every
day since 1991, when he left us, Allah y rahmou. *I miss Dad so much!*

Beyond the fact that we never talk about him, I think it's sad we've
never visited his grave together. That's been a dream of mine that will
hopefully be realized not too long from now. February 2, 1991 was and
remains the blackest day of my life. You were home sleeping that day,
and I was at a friend of mine's.

I've always wondered how that day was for him.

I've never told you this, but I'd like to share it with you. I was with
a friend named Indio. We had fun that night—some laughing, some
chillin'! We ended up watching a movie, and I really liked it.

That movie seems to have a message that, I swear on my son, proved
to be a tragic message the following morning.

It was about two young guys—a Black one and a white one (Indio
and Aziz). These two were best friends and shared everything togeth-
er. They got into trouble, pulled pranks. The father of the white boy
gets sick, and it gnaws at him.

Our father, Allah y rahmou, *wasn't sick; he was very strong. But*
I think he was unhappy after the divorce from Mom. I even think he
had regrets, Allah y rahmou.

Back to the movie: the father of the white boy gets sicker and sicker.
I recognize myself in him. A rebellious boy. And then suddenly, the
news comes that his father has passed away!!

The movie touched and moved me, so I went to bed and slept over, rather than coming home. The following morning, someone came to the door, and it turned out to be Danouche's son, Mounir!

I went to the door, and when he saw me, his first words were: "Your father is dead." My words were: "If you're lying, I'll kill you!!" I pulled my clothes on, held his hand, and ran home! As soon as I got back, I went crazy and ran away. Dad wasn't there anymore— Mounir didn't lie.

The first thing that came to my mind was the movie from the night before!!!

I immediately google the movie and find *Big Shots* from 1987. That must be it. The movie is about Obie, a twelve-year-old boy who moves from his comfortable house in the suburbs to the rough South Side of Chicago after the death of his father. There, he's befriended by Scam, a scam artist who's his age. Together, they have wild adventures, stealing a Mercedes with a corpse in the trunk. Amid all of the funny criminal escapades, there's a serious undertone. Scam grew up without a father. Obie promises to help him make contact with his father, which is his way of working through his own loss.

When our father blew his last breath, all of us spun out in different directions. I ended up writing and drawing; Aziz ended up with the guys on the streets; Jamal and Nourdin ended up on the soccer field. I wonder where Malika and Pascal ended up? Would it have helped if we talked more? Would things have gone differently then? Or is this just how life is? Everyone has to make the best of things in their own way and take responsibility for it.

Reading this letter, I understand so much better why Aziz does what he does. Would they understand me if I told them about myself? I sometimes think of calling everyone together, but I don't know if I have the courage. I won't be able to say aloud what's happened anyway. Suppose I tell them, and they show compassion—isn't that what I really want?

A while ago, I wrote a blog about this question. "When does a victim get our compassion?" When does one feel another's pain? Some people I know support Palestinians, but not LGBT people. Some care about victims of extremist Muslims, but not about victims of Western drones. The question came up because in social media posts of family members, friends, and acquaintances, I see a lot of attention devoted toward Islamophobia and racism, but little toward the oppression of sexual minorities. They discriminate with their compassion.

"If the perpetrator fits our image of the enemy, then we scream bloody murder. But if the victim looks more like 'the other,' we hide behind trivializing and hypocritical words."

Indirectly, the blog is about me. I want to know if the communities that I belong to will develop compassion for people like me. In my inbox, in response to the blog post, I get an email from a student who's working on a thesis about the subject.

Dear Tofik Dibi,

Based on what's happening now, your question about compassion is at the front of my mind.

You can be not only a victim of discrimination, but also be discriminated against as a victim. That's what I'm writing my thesis on, more or less. It's interesting that when we rationally make an equal judgment about the seriousness of two different situations, we still find one more important than the other. Compassion probably goes primarily to the victim who looks the most like us, because that situation increases our fear that the same thing could happen to us. And fear is useful: we resist it. I find it impressive when people express compassion even when it doesn't produce "useful" fear (I'm thinking of vegetarians, for example). In my view, most people neutralize the pain of others.

It makes me think of the debate about Mauro. At the age of nine, he came alone from Angola to the Netherlands, where he was taken in by a foster family. When he turned eighteen, he was threatened with deportation. Lots of people revolted in protest against the deportation, not only in his immediate community, but beyond. Even a surprisingly large number of PVV sympathizers believed that Mauro had the right to a residency permit. As hard as local and national politicians, children's rights organizations like Defense for Children, and both famous and everyday Dutch people supported him, I'm convinced that there was ultimately one decisive factor: Mauro himself.

In our debate about immigration, people speak with their fingers in their ears and listen with their eyes shut. Everything changes when a political debate becomes a human being. There was a face and a voice, and that's why people could put themselves in his shoes. People can learn to have compassion for someone who doesn't look like them at first glance. Mauro's case proves this, but it's impossible without seeing a face, hearing a voice, and knowing the story.

"Dibi!"

"Hey man."

"You're really killing it, boss."

"*Soukran.*"

"You speak really well."

I always have to laugh when I hear that. Of all the things that people say to me in public, this is the undisputed frontrunner. Still. Without exception, it's minority youth, usually Moroccan-Dutch boys, who say it. It's ironic, really: however good I am with words, the thing I really want to speak about is stuck in my mouth.

15

I'm going to interview three imams who also have *it* for VICE Netherlands, where I'm interning. I pitched the idea after meeting one of them, Muhsin Hendricks, at a recent get-together of the Dutch Turkish Workers Association. He said things that I don't dare believe, things I've hopelessly longed for. I'm hesitant to open the Koran to look for the specific verses. I know the translation and the popular interpretation of the story of the prophet Lot, but I've never dared to analyze the literal words. Allah only knows how many lives have been mutilated, destroyed by these words. Allah only knows how many are still to follow.

What if they mean what I've always hoped they mean—what am I going to do then?

I have the numbers of the verses lined up, and I have a translated copy of the Koran and online Dutch translations open in front of me. Like a weapons inspector, I start searching the texts for the possible presence of words of mass destruction. It takes hours before I comprehend the chronology and the story, because the verses are spread over different chapters, called *surahs*.

The city of Sodom is a cesspool. The inhabitants besiege, rob, and murder passing travelers. Men are raped in public without shame. Allah therefore directs the prophet Lot, the nephew of the prophet Ibrahim, to call on the people of Sodom to better their lives. Lot tries his absolute hardest, but the people are deaf to his sermons. When he warns the inhabitants about being punished by Allah, they still ignore him. They threaten to banish him from the city if he keeps preaching.

Lot continues to proclaim Allah's message, without success. Even within his own household, not everyone follows the word of God—his wife is an unbeliever. Lot prays desperately to Allah for salvation from the immorality that plagues Sodom. In response, Allah sends three angels to Sodom. Lot's young daughter is the first to see the group as they arrive. She's fascinated by their purity.

Lot asks them where they've come from and where they're going. They don't answer his questions, but rather ask for shelter. Lot is concerned for them, telling them about the unhinged inhabitants. He asks them to wait until it's dark so that they won't be seen and nothing will happen to them. When Lot welcomes them into his house, his wife secretly sneaks out the door. She runs to the townspeople and tells them about the three unusual guests. Excited, they rush to the home of Lot, who is taken by surprise. When he can't find his wife, he realizes how the news has spread.

Before the crowd arrives at his house, he locks the door. They bang on the door. Lot begs them to leave the guests in peace and to fear Allah, who will surely punish them if they have their way with the men, while also having wives.

7 Surah "The Elevated Places"—Al-A'raf

80 "And Lot, when he said to his people: 'Do you commit an atrocity such as no one before you in the world hath committed?'"

81 "You approach men with desire, instead of women. No, thou art a people who transgress beyond the limits."

They laugh at him and break down the door. Lot keeps speaking to the intruders, but it doesn't help.

The guests calm him by revealing that they are angels. When the crowd hears this, they flee in terror while making threats against Lot. The angels warn Lot. He must leave his house and the city before sunrise with his entire family, with the exception of his wife. Allah has commanded that Sodom be destroyed.

54 Surah "The Moon"—Al-Qamar
    34 "Indeed, We sent a storm of stones down upon them all, with the exception of Lot's family, whom we saved before dawn."

An earthquake turns the city upside down, and stones thunder down from the sky. Everything and everyone is destroyed. The story told in the verses of the chapter "The Elevated Places" is recalled again in chapter 26.

26 Surah "The Poets"—Ash-Shu'ara
    165 "Do you approach men, among all the creatures?"
    166 "And do you leave your women, whom your Lord has created for you? No, thou art a people transgressing beyond the limits."

I read the verses again. And over and over again. I look at the different translations and the interpretations. Even if I play devil's advocate, with a passion, I can't find any judgment about sexual orientation or love between two men. This is about rape and other immoral, uncontrolled behavior. The crowd at Lot's door wants to assault the angels Gabriel, Michael, and Israphael. And even if the verses were actually about sexual orientation, the intervention and punishment come unequivocally from Allah, not from humans.

Nor do the stories about the life of the Prophet—the *sunnah*—contain any general, reliable texts in which the prophet Mohammed considers homosexuality to be punishable. When I delve deeper into this and call up an expert, I learn that even within the four schools of thought within Islam, there are different interpretations. According to Abu Hanifa, the spiritual father of the Hanafi school, there is no officially recognized punishment for *Louata*, which stands for people who do what the people in the Book of Lot do. The other schools connect punishments to the disruption of public order through public homosexual deeds. What two people do with each other in private can be a sin in this case, but the rules of punishment, according to the Koran, do not apply here. This is underscored by the fact that four witnesses must be called before a punishment can be decreed.

For the VICE interview I email and call the French-Algerian imam Ludovic-Mohamed Zahed, imam Daayiee Abdullah from Washington, DC, and the South African imam Muhsin Hendricks. When I ask Hendricks what he discovered when he studied the verses, he confirms roughly what I think.

"I found that the Koran says nothing about sexual orientation. The story about Sodom and Gomorrah is about atrocities like rape, robbery, exploitation, and inhospitality. Once I knew that, I realized that it is not God, but rather the people who interpret the Koran who are homophobic. At that moment, I felt free to be completely myself."

The other two imams use other words but come to the same conclusion as Hendricks. Or am I, and are we, reading into it what we want to read, out of self-interest? However meticulously I unpack every letter, every word, every verse, every *surah*, every translation, examining them closely, words of mass destruction are nowhere to be found. This gives me strength. I am exhilarated that I don't have to give up Allah. At the same time, this isn't only about the interpretation of the Koran. The religious message in movies, TV series, books, and songs in which Adam and Eve are idolized is imprinted just as strongly in my brain. In the end, does it really matter what the Koran exactly says if the majority of Muslims thinks otherwise? Do the people defending the popular interpretations even care that they might be completely wrong? How can I start a conversation about this in a time when Islam is criticized five times a day? The "criticism" is mostly Muslim-hate disguised with a wig, phony mustache, and fake glasses. How can I get *them* to speak calmly about *it* when we're constantly being targeted? When it's not Muslim-hate in disguise, it's plain old racism, under the pretense of "giving the people a voice," as in the tavern in The Hague where Geert Wilders addresses his supporters.

"And I can't really say it out loud, because then I'll be reported to the police. And maybe there are even D66 officers who'll charge me. But freedom of expression is a wonderful thing. And we're not saying anything that's not allowed. We haven't said anything that isn't true. So, I'm asking you: do you want more Moroccans in this city, or fewer?"

"Fewer! Fewer! Fewer! Fewer! Fewer!"

The room claps and cheers. Martin Bosma happily joins in.

"Okay ... we're going to make sure that happens."

I immediately start writing a second open letter to PVV voters. I did it before as an MP. When I look at the first letter again, I'm annoyed at how defensive and reactive I was.

> Not one hair on my head fantasizes for a single second about the introduction of Sharia or about violent jihad. Every time I see a burka, I experience it as a walking prison, just like you. Gay people must be able to walk hand in hand in our streets without anyone raising their fists against them. Cabaret performers, columnists, authors, and artists must be able to criticize Islam freely without fearing for their lives.

Now it's different.

> As an MP, I did my very best to listen to your concerns and to do something about them, but this time it's you who needs to listen.
>
> You are not a victim.
>
> Maybe your life isn't what you hoped for. Maybe you've experienced injustice. And maybe you see others who appear to have more than you. But that is no excuse.
>
> You are a fully fledged adult who consciously chooses to vote for a racist party. Does that make you a racist? I don't know. But it sure makes you complicit with racism.
>
> Once, I told your political leader that I understand that the arrival

and permanent residence of immigrants, including Muslims, can feel like a forced marriage. You can divorce from marriage, as painful as it is. But when there are children, the bond is permanent, and a good relationship is in everyone's interest.

My nephews and nieces are some of these children. Soon, when you pick up that red pencil and give your vote to the PVV, know that you are telling them that they are inferior.

You are completely responsible for that. No one else.

When my parents used to grab the sandal to punish me and my brothers for making a mess at home, it was because they considered the house to be our collective responsibility. What's been happening for more than ten years now is something different. It is as if my father and mother were not only punishing us, but went around to all of the families in Vlissingen, in the Netherlands, in the world to give all the people who look like us a good beating. In the Netherlands, everyone is an individual, unless he or she is dark-skinned. Then the Enlightenment is suddenly suspended, and "we" all look like each other.

A little after midnight, I'm walking home, because I missed the last tram. At the end of Kinkerstraat, close to my old internet hangout, a Vespa scooter is coming my way. The driver is a boy. He sees and recognizes me, and he yells at the top of his lungs.

"Homo! Faggot! *Zemel!*"

I stop, turn around, and vaguely hear him beating his chest, but he doesn't stop. No more than a couple minutes later, I see another Moroccan-Dutch guy walking toward me. He's wearing a track suit, just like the other guy. He recognizes me too.

"Dibiiii! How's it going? We're proud of you, man!"

16

Even before he starts to cry, I feel him about to wake me from my sleep. Since his arrival, *it* has been dispelled. When I say his name, Lhoucine—after my father—to soothe him, he babbles sounds from answered prayers. Everything has gone so fast: the wedding in Morocco, the birth, the move. My whole family was there, and my best friends flew in. When Firdaus and I were lifted together in an *amaria*—a sort of mobile throne—by my four brothers, wearing traditional dress, and carried through the room, I saw my mother among the merriment. She saw that things were good.

I had to. Really, it's a simple calculation—a question of adding and subtracting. If I'd chosen *it*, my Moroccan-ness, my manhood, and my religion would have been taken from me. I would be left alone with *it*. Now, the only thing I've lost is *it*. While I give Lhoucine his bottle, sleeping sounds infiltrate the dream. It's not Firdaus.

It's Fouad who's woken me abruptly with his snoring. He's lying next to me in my grandma's house. The same dream, again. We partied until the wee hours of the morning. My cousin Abdellah got married yesterday. In the coming weeks, two other cousins, Hayat and Naima, are getting married. The preparations are taking place all around me. While I'm tapping away on my MacBook, family members are coming and going. They keep asking me why I'm staying inside so much. I've observed Ramadan here and am staying until the last wedding. My grandma's house, where I'm staying, is being used as a storage room. The fridge is jam-packed with ingredients for the wedding feasts; over a hundred roasted chickens and a hundred kilos of meat have been ordered. Everywhere I look, I see crates of fruit-flavored soda and cola, huge plates of cookies; kaftans and suits. They're whispering.

We can be there for you, too.

While I'm typing, my eyes keep falling on the Arabic calligraphy that's hanging across from me on the wall. It was a gift from my mother to my grandma. It is the *shahada* in the shape of a praying boy. This boy doesn't consist of the words that others say about him. He defines himself. I'm going to visit my grandma's grave this morning with my uncle Si el-Arbi before it gets too hot. She passed away two years ago. At the grave, my uncle will lead us in the ceremonial prayers. On his knees, he recites long verses tirelessly. I wonder how he interprets the story of the prophet Lot, but I know that I'll never know the answer. I'm curious if he'll hear what I've been up to—rumors spread like wildfire here. Fouad reads verses aloud from the Koran that he's brought along. I whisper along with the verses that I know by heart.

Luckily she's not here anymore.

That's *them.* They are trying to scare me.

If she were still alive and knew what you were planning, she'd never look at you or talk to you again.

During lunch, my aunts seize their opportunity again. I see photos of Muslim women who look like them constantly in the negative news reports about Muslims, especially about the oppression of women. These days, my aunts are like dictators. They decide how the weddings unfold, which music will be played, what will be eaten and served, who's on the guest list, and what the dowry is. They're still at ease with me, but I don't mind anymore. It means that they see me as one of them, and I am—no matter what happens.

"How old are you now?"

"Thirty-four."

"And still not married? Isn't it time?"

"No...."

"Why not?"

I sigh theatrically.

"I'm busy with other things right now."

"Just say the word. We can match you with a good girl."

"Ha ha ha.... I'd like to choose for myself."

A relay race of raised eyebrows follows.

"God forbid you pick a Dutch woman! And the wedding will be here, not in the Netherlands!"

I laugh. They're persistent. When they're getting nowhere with me, they take an alternate route via my mother.

"And when will that parliamentarian of yours, Chinoui, get married?" Chinoui is my nickname: Chinese.

She doesn't answer right away, glances at me, and smiles.

"*El alem Allah.*" Only Allah knows.

All of the things I've never said, all of the things I wanted to hear, lie in that hesitation, that glance, her smile and intonation.

I don't know for sure, but she must be having a hard time these days with three kids of her sisters' getting married. I would have loved to give her that—a wedding here between her son and his bride, something that she could also show off with.

Today it's Hayat's turn. Hayat took great care of my grandma, and I helped her as much as I could with everything. Before evening, when the festivities begin in a large tent, I'm diving into the feast with the other male guests. First there's roast chicken with olives and preserved lemons, and then beef with plums. There are ten men at my table. I'm ready this time. At an earlier wedding, I turned around to grab some bread from another table. When I turned back, there were only chicken bones left.

"*Tfou!*"

Fouad is in a heated conversation with a couple of our friends and others at the table. They've heard a rumor. The singer from a wedding band has been caught with a catering server. The server is a boy.

"Why would a man be with another man when there's an abundance of women?"

"Do you see what the world is coming to?"

They try to pull me into the conversation. I've often been a witness to this kind of talk, here and in the Netherlands. Sometimes I've gone along with the disdain, but I don't have it in me anymore.

"Everyone should live the way they want to live. I don't judge. I leave that to Allah."

They quiet down and stare at me.

"You foreigners have a different mentality."

I see some of the guests at the table examining me. They're looking for *it*. That look—I've often witnessed that too. I used to look away nervously to hide myself, but I don't want that anymore.

"You yourselves do plenty of things that are seen as haram."

It gets quiet again.

"Don't talk about how much you love Allah—show it by how you treat all of his creatures."

Before Naima's wedding, the third and last wedding, I'm going to honor my father's family. It's about thirteen hours by car to Guelmim, "the gateway to the Sahara." Fouad is coming along. The closer we get, the more the date palms are like welcome signs coming out of the dry plains. The loam houses all look like each other, but we find our destination on our first try. It's as if Allah blew away decades of layers of desert sand with one soft breath to unveil the footprints of my younger self to show the way. There is the big steel blue door. We used to shoot at doves with catapults for grilling, and my cousin Fatma once killed a stray snake here with a herding stick. The house is still as big; the garden just as studded with pomegranates, cactus fruits, figs, and grapes; the stable just as filled with the bleating and clucking of goats and chickens. The only thing missing is the people. Only my aunt Aicha is still alive; she lives here with my mentally ill cousin el-Bechir. The first thing she does when she sees me is grab perfume to spray on us. Fouad tries to maneuver around the perfume as much as possible. He says that you get gray hair from the perfume. Then she makes "Moroccan whiskey." I spend hours asking her about my father's youth. She tells me that he used to always gossip with his aunts and cousins, just like I do. At no point do I think about grabbing my phone or laptop—we keep talking until we fall asleep outside under the starry sky, exhausted from the heat. No stars fall from the sky.

The next day, we get up extra early to go to my father's grave. The graveyard is just behind the garden, about a five-minute walk. It's almost fifty degrees Celsius, making breathing difficult, but I feel recharged. Most of the graves are anonymous, but I immediately recognize his resting place. I feel a hint of bitterness welling up, because he was flown immediately to Morocco after his death and we couldn't come along. Luckily my mother went along to bury him here. Fouad begins to recite verses, and I follow his example. A loose stone on the grave catches my attention. I pick it up and put it in my pocket to take back home with me.

"I wasn't at your burial, but when I'm buried, you'll be there. I will lie right here next to you."

Fouad looks at me the same way that I looked at him at the grave of our grandma. He wants to see if I'm crying. No tears. I'm anything but sad.

"Give me a sign if I shouldn't do this, Dad. Please."

I look at the bunched dates on the palms to see if maybe a date, in some mysterious fashion, manages to fall, unripe, on the ground. Nothing happens.

"I drink Moroccan whiskey now too. Now you know, in case we ever watch movies together again."

Before we return for Naima's wedding, I look for my father's favorite cousin. She isn't home. Her husband is there, with an older man I don't know. As I walk toward him to give him a kiss on his head and hand, I hear him say something. I never learned the Berber language Tashelhiyt—we speak Moroccan Arabic—but I manage to understand this much.

"This is Lhoucine's son."

Immediately after the greeting, I hurry to the bathroom. I have no idea why, but tears come out. He saw my father in me. After a tajine with goat meat, my least favorite, Fouad and I pack our things and say our goodbyes.

"Please tell the other sons and the daughter of Lhoucine that we'd like to see them too."

After a sweaty, thirteen-hour drive back, with many watermelon breaks along the way, we arrive at my grandma's house. It's still just as crowded. Kids from the neighborhood are standing by the door, staring at their smartphones. I had wifi installed in order to be able to write and gave them the password. If they stand close enough to the door, they get a connection too. The curiosity about what I'm doing day and night on my MacBook is reaching a climax.

"Read us something from that book."

"It's in Dutch."

"Then translate it for us."

"Don't be annoying—I'm busy."

Every family member who comes in and sees me writing makes me ask myself the same questions.

Will you still greet me when you hear about it?

Will I see you the next time, or is this the last time?

How will Ussama and the guys in the hookah lounge react?

After Naima's wedding, I get ready to go back to the Netherlands. My mother is staying a while longer.

"Tawfiq."

"Yes?"

"Your book … you're not writing anything about me, right? I'm warning you."

"No, Mama."

"Nothing about me, Tawfiq."

"I've already told you—the book is about my life."

"I won't talk to you anymore if you write something about me."

"Don't worry, Mama, really. You're not even mentioned in the book."

"Okay."

She looks at me and thinks for a moment.

"What's it about?"

"Just things. The things I've experienced."

"What kinds of things have you experienced?"

"Just things. Politics. And other things."

"..."

She knows. She knows that I know that she knows. And she is still here. That is enough for me—that is everything.

I wake up well before I need to leave for the airport in Casablanca. It's six thirty, and the sun is still warming up. Since I've been in Morocco, I've thought about going to take a look. It's been more than twenty years. I put my jogging pants on and tiptoe out the door so that Fouad and my mother don't hear me. There's hardly anyone on the street. There it is—the magical cave. Even if I knew for sure that it would work, I wouldn't do it. To dispel *it* would mean to dispel Allah.

Once I'm back in the Netherlands, I take the tram to Henk to rummage around in the boxes of comics and see what I find. Raindrops, the hint of weed, and the smell of fries with mayonnaise welcome me back while I walk through the alleyways to the Zeedijk. I maneuver around drunk and stoned tourists and ignore hissing dealers until I'm standing surrounded by the comics. I'm home. And yet it's never been so hard to leave Morocco as it was this time. I'm worried that soon everything will be different.

I never feel so strongly Dutch as when I'm in Morocco, and never so completely Moroccan as when I'm in the Netherlands. Not until I was in Parliament did I feel so Muslim, and never do I feel so political as when I profess my faith. I never see myself as more of a monster than when I'm sitting among Moroccans and Muslims and never feel so Moroccan and Muslim as when I feel *it*. Morocco, the Netherlands, my religion, *it* and *they*: none has been expelled, nor have they made peace. Not yet. As much as I tried, suppressed, prayed, fled, and wandered, nothing brought salvation. But there is still one thing that I haven't explored.

They say that monsters have no reflection in the mirror, because a mirror reveals the soul, and monsters are soulless creatures. *They* say a lot. Monsters are created when people don't allow themselves to have a face and a voice. Mirrors can't reflect what is devoured by self-hate. Because that is what *it* and *they* were this whole time: hatred toward myself.

I'm going to try: to stand in front of a mirror, as myself.

Acknowledgments

First and foremost, always, Allah, *Subhanahu Wa Ta'ala*. Every time I think of You, You think of me. I can never express how much You mean to me.

Mama, Malika, Pascal, Jamal, Aziz, Fouad, and Nourdin: forgive me. I know this will cause you pain, but don't worry: whatever comes, it will never match up to what has been.

My three coreaders, Christel, Noortje, and Femke: I couldn't have done this without you.

You don't know the half of how special you are, Christel. Sometimes I like that, because it makes you grounded. More often, I think it's too bad, because you are more valuable than you know.

Noortje: I remember how we were introduced to each other like it was yesterday: MP and policy staff—two "pipsqueaks" who eagerly wanted to make the world a better place. I look forward to experiencing many more adventures together.

Those curls of yours, Femke—I know that you're not religious, but how coincidental is it that your hair is so symbolic of your indomitable personality? I have learned so unbelievably much from you. Thank you.

Mustafa Ayranci, *amca*! Every time I hear you speak, I want to storm the barricades. I love you.

Mohammed Rabbae, Si Mohammed! You are my hero. I am eternally grateful to you.

Mai, you mysterious being, I want to thank you for your tenacity and your quirkiness. That means so much to me.

Job, Ronit, and Sabine, I want to thank you for your expertise.

Special thanks to editor Rebecca Colesworthy and series editors Cynthia Burack and Jyl J. Josephson for your enthusiasm, and to the entire SUNY Press staff.

Nick, thank you so much for helping me to reach my brothers and sisters beyond borders. I will never forget it.